*F-105.*

# Magic 100

## The story of an F-105,
## 100 Combat Mission tour, NVN '67

### by Al Lenski

Turner Publishing Company

# Turner Publishing Company
## The Front Line of Military History Books

Author: Al Lenski, BG (Ret.) USAF
Cover art by Harley Copic

Library of Congress
Catalog Card No.  95-070513

ISBN: 978-1-68162-319-1

Limited Edition

# Table of Contents

# Acknowledgment

I'd like to thank artist, Mr. Harley Copic, for allowing Turner Publishing Company to use his painting "Thunder over the Red River" on the cover of this book. It realistically captures what it really looked like as F-105 flights roll in for a bomb run on a target near the Red River and Thud Ridge in Route Package 6, North Vietnam.

I regret not writing this book earlier so that my late brother, Larry, would have had a chance to read this story. Larry was an Air Force Intelligence Officer during the Korean War and truly understood the frustrations of flying combat under the restrictions in the air war over North Vietnam and kept in frequent contact with me with letter and tapes throughout my tour. His understanding and concern for my safety encouraged me to endure these frustrations.

Most importantly, I want to dedicate this book to my wife, Bettye, and my four children: Diane, Carol, Randy, and Mark. Bettye, for hanging in there during those seven months of my tour which had to be agonizing, not knowing if or when a blue Air Force staff car might come visiting unexpectedly with some bad news. For the kids, for being patient and understanding the frustrations that their mother was going through while she filled the role of both mother and father.

Lastly, I want to thank all those Wingmen and Flight Lead warriors I flew with during my tour who gave mutual support not only in the heat of battle, but in a personal manner when the going tough and emotions ran high. Thanks, guys, for all the memories!

*Brig. General Al Lenski, author*

# The Charge of the Flight Brigade
## (To Get Their One Hundred)
### Composed in 1967-8th TFW

Twenty clicks, twenty clicks,
twenty clicks onward,
All in the valley of Death
   They flew their one hundred
     *When can their glory fade?*

"Forward the Flight Brigade!
Dive onthose guns!" he said
Into the valley of Death
   They flew their one hundred.
     *O the wild flights they made!*

"Forward the Flight Brigade!"
Was there a man dismay'd?
Not tho' the pilots knew
Someone had blunder'd.
Theirs not to reason why,
Their but to fight and fly.
Into the valley of Death
   They flew their one hundred.
     *All the world wonder'd.*

Flak to the right of them
Flak to the left of them.
Flak in front of them
Volley'd and thunder'd;
Storm'd at with SAM and shell,
Boldly they flew and well,
Into the jaws of Death,
Into the mouth of hell
   They flew their one hundred.
     *Honor the flights they made?*

Flashed all their sparrows bare,
Flashed as they turned in air,
Strafing the gunners there,
Charging a nation, while
   All the world ponder'd.
     *Honor the Flight Brigade.*

Plunged in the trip-A smoke
Right thro' the Migs they broke,
Chinese and Russian
Reel'd from the Sparrow-stroke
   Shatter'd and sunder'd
Then they rode back, but not,
   All got their hundred.
     *Noble one hundred!*

Flak to the right of them,
Flak to the left of them,
Flak behind them
   Volley'd and thunder'd;
Storm'd at with SAM and shell,
While planes and pilots fell,
They who had fought so well
Came thro' the jaws of Death
Back from the mouth of hell
   All that was left of them
     *To get their one hundred.*

# Introduction

Flying 100 combat missions into North Vietnam in 1967 was a ticket home, a completed remote tour of duty. Normally, a remote tour was 12 months, so this was a policy change. This change seemed to be the result of the heavy losses sustained by the pilots who flew up north early on in the Air war, particularly during the "Rolling Thunder" campaign, as the North Vietnamese air defenses increased in effectiveness, sophistication and numbers.

The North Vietnam air defenses consisted mainly of mixed heavy anti-aircraft-artillery (AAA) 37 Millimeter (MM), 57MM, 85MM and 100MM, Migs, Surface-to-Air-Missiles (SAMs) and small arms fire at low altitude. All of these defenses were concentrated in a very small geographic area surrounding Hanoi. In 1967, Hanoi had become the most heavily defended city on earth. North Vietnam possessed approximately 200 SAM sites, 7,000 antiaircraft guns, a sophisticated ground-controlled intercept (GCI) system and about 80 Migs. Most of these defenses were located in the heartland of the Red River delta.

This area was known as route package six, where railroad yards, sidings, steel mills, power plants, factories and supply routes were prime targets for U.S. air strikes. One pilot in every 40 who flew over the Red River never came back. All told, North Vietnamese defenses downed 326 American aircraft during 1967.

Thuds were the work-horse fighter-bombers used during the Rolling Thunder bombing campaign over North Vietnam in 1964-1968. More than 240 Thuds were shot down during Rolling Thunder. Eighty-seven of those were lost during 1967.

Although Migs and SAMs were not a big threat in the lower parts of North Vietnam (south of Hanoi), AAA was usually intense and concentrated along major supply routes where the majority of our air strikes were scheduled. It was realized that pilots flying missions into those defenses, at the rate we did, for a 12 month period would make surviving a combat tour almost impossible. A decision was made therefore, to limit the number of missions crews would fly up north to "100". This would then allow the pilots to be credited with a complete tour of duty. The normal 12 month tour was still the policy for those pilots flying less than 100 missions north or for those only flying in South Vietnam.

So surviving 100 missions in a combat crew role in the north had taken on a new meaning. Survive 100 missions up north, and you won't have to stay for a full 12 months. It meant a ticket home! Like magic! This sounded like a quick way to complete a tour, but the odds weren't that great, so there were some variations to this policy. Twenty (20) missions up north could be credited for one month curtailment from the normal 12 months. Any combination of months and missions which added up to 12 months by that formula was considered a completed tour. For example, if a pilot flew 80 missions and had served at least 8 months, the tour was considered complete. On average, during the 1967 time-frame, an F-105 pilot would fly about 20 missions a month up north. Most pilots wanted to complete 100 missions since this could be accomplished in about 6 months. During my six and one half months in early '67, flying enough missions was not a problem. Surviving those 100 missions was.

# Rules of Engagement (ROE) - Vietnam

In order to understand the frustrations of the fighter pilot during the Rolling Thunder bombing campaign against North Vietnam, some background about the rules of engagement that restricted the scope of fighting and imposed unrealistic limitations on U.S. forces during the Vietnam War.

In an April 15, 1985 issue of the Air Force Times, an article appeared by a Times Staff Writer that discussed two declassified Air Force studies released by Sen. Barry Goldwater (R-Ariz.) on the "rules of engagement" or combat limitations, imposed on U.S. forces during the Vietnam War. This studies were published in the March 14 and March 26 issues of the Congressional Record. Sen. Goldwater, chairman of the Senate Armed Services Committee, at the time, made the following charges as a result of these released studies. "With civilian 'amateurs' in the Pentagon and the State Department directing day-to-day fighting in Vietnam in 1966, U.S. bombers were allowed to hit less than 10 percent of 242 prime targets in North Vietnam selected by the Joint Chiefs of Staff."

The first study examined rules of engagement used from 1960 to 1965. The second covers 1966 to 1969 and reports on disagreements between military leaders and President Johnson and his Defense secretary, Robert S. McNamara, over the scope of fighting and the limitations imposed on the air warfare.

Goldwater also released a bombing policy paper prepared in 1968 by then-Chairman of the Joint Chiefs of Staff Gen. Earle G. Wheeler. It suggested closing the port of Haiphong and other North Vietnamese seaports with mines and lifting restrictions on bombing certain areas, including Hanoi and Haiphong. Goldwater said Wheeler never formally recommended these changes to McNamara because he had been told that President Johnson would not consider them.

Under the rules of engagement, the Air Force's "Rolling Thunder" bombing program was aimed at stopping North Vietnamese supplies and soldiers moving south, not at destroying staging areas in the north. This policy was constantly reviewed by the commander in chief Pacific and by the Joint Chiefs but no changes took place. According to Goldwater, even Congress criticized this policy in 1967.

In an August 1967 congressional hearing, former Sen. Margaret C. Smith (R-Maine) questioned McNamara about the rules of engagement, saying the air war restrictions were increasing U.S. casualties in the south.

McNamara rejected the notion and said that mining North Vietnam harbors might bring a direct confrontation with the Soviet Union.

The report noted that two months earlier U.S. aircraft mistakenly attacked the Soviet merchant ship, Turkestan, 40 kilometers north of Haiphong. (As a personal note, Since I was one of 20 other pilots who participated on this mission, the Turkestan was not "mistakenly" attacked. The Soviet ship, located in the port of Cam Pha, initiated the attack on a flight of F-105s as we exited Pack 6 after bombing a target on the northeast railroad. The F-105 flight responded in kind by strafing the ship that fired on them as permitted by the current rules of engagement, as we pilots understood it. Col Broughton's (acting 355 TFW Commander at the time of the incident) book, "Going Downtown, The War Against Hanoi and Washington" relates the real story of this incident in great detail since Col Broughton, and Maj Ted Tolman (the pilot who strafed the Turkestan and Maj Lonnie Ferguson, his wingman) all faced Court Martial charges for this incident.

The released reports however indicate that events such as the Turkestan attack frequently led to changes in air war rules of engagement in Laos and North and South Vietnam. These events were referred to as "Short Round" incidents and considered to be errant air attacks on civilians. However, they had their greatest restrictive effect on the covert air war over Laos, which was controlled by the U.S. ambassador in the Laotian capitol at Vientiane. The ambassador, with limited or no military experience, controlled ordnance, target validation, defoliation, prisoner camp restrictions and ground forward air control personnel.

The report states that on average, it took six to eight days to obtain clearance from Vientiane to conduct an air strike, although in some cases, armed reconnaissance flights were permitted to fire on ground forces if they were first attacked. In southern Laos, where the enemy carried supplies and reinforcement into South Vietnam along the Ho Chi Minh Trail, the delay in obtaining clearance, and other rules, allowed the enemy to escape U.S. attack continually after Americans discovered their presence.

For at least two years, the military strictly followed the rule that no force in Laos could be attacked if it was more than 200 yards from a "motorable" road, the report said. Finally, in 1969, the U.S. ambassador in Vientiane told American commanders they could pursue forces beyond 200 yards into a hiding area, because, he reasoned, the path used to reach a hiding area was 'de facto" motorable.

Goldwater said the prohibition against bombing Hanoi or Haiphong transformed both cities into importing centers for war material from other communist countries.

Besides the "sanctuaries" established in Hanoi and Haiphong, U.S. pilots were prohibited from striking near temples and other Vietnamese historic structures. This provided more sanctuaries, some close to the South Vietnamese border, which were used as staging areas for troops and supplies, the Air Force analysts said.

It appears that the restrictions on the American air war in Vietnam had their roots in the early days of U.S. involvement, when President portrayed the U.S. role as advisory. But other information in the Air Force study indicated the United States may have agreed with China not to lift certain geographic and procedural restrictions on bombing missions as the war intensified.

(McNamara, in a January 1967 hearing on Capitol Hill, denied that such an agreement existed.)

On March 31, 1968, President Johnson ordered a halt to the bombing of North Vietnam and announced that he would not seek a second full term. On April 2, air attacks into North Vietnam stopped. Hot-pursuit flights against enemy fighters no longer were authorized. U.S. ships in the Gulf of Tonkin had to remain in international waters. The study said, "Thus ended the Rolling Thunder program. The Chief Executive had placed outside the reach of American air power precisely that area which military judgment considered to be the most essential to strike."

The bombing halt also affected the air war over Laos and South Vietnam. A buffer zone had to be created 10 miles outside the North Vietnamese border to prevent errant attacks on North Vietnam.

Goldwater concluded with, "Our pilots and fighting men had to memorize every tiniest detail of these complicated and lengthy rules and implement them under extreme moments of stress. If anyone ever again foolishly criticizes the performance of our military in the Vietnam War, after having read these rules, he or she must not understand the English language."

Sen. Goldwater's assessment of this report, in 1985, only confirmed what the pilots who flew missions into North Vietnam during Rolling Thunder knew then, but, right or wrong, like all dedicated military soldiers and airmen, we fought by the rules our leaders asked us to follow - even though we knew this was not the way this war should be fought if you want to win.

# Chapter One
# *Leaving For A Combat Tour (NVN)*

One of the hardest and most painful things about this tour was preparing myself for leaving my family while knowing that the chances and odds of surviving 100 missions in an F-105 combat tour were poor. The odds of seeing them again, I thought, were pretty slim. I had been married to Bettye for 13 years by Jan, '67 with two daughters, ages 13 and 12, and two sons, one 10 yrs and the youngest, 15 mos.

Following my graduation and receiving a B.A. at the University of Iowa in '52, I also received my commission in the Air Force as a second lieutenant through the R.O.T.C. program with orders to class 53-F for "Primary" pilot training starting in August of that year at Hondo A.B., Texas. I was really happy to have qualified for pilot training and was looking forward to the new experiences of not just the military but flying airplanes. I spent the first couple of months after graduation in June '52 playing baseball at Mason City, Iowa where I pitched for the "Mason City Legionnaires" of the Iowa State semi-professional baseball league. This was my second baseball season with them and I knew that I'd have to leave the end of July before the season was over to report for pilot training with the Air Force. For me, it would be the end of a long career of playing baseball at this level and I hated for it to end. Baseball had been my life until now. Little did I know that I was about to embark on a 30 year career with the Air Force flying fighter airplanes and enjoying the hell out of it.

I met my wife, Bettye, at Bryan AFB, Texas where I was assigned for basic pilot training following six months of T-6 primary flying training at Hondo A.B., Texas. Bettye and I met at the officers club during the later part of my pilot training, then continued our relationship after my follow on assignment to Perrin AFB, Texas for advanced fighter training in the F-86D. I'd commute to see her at Bryan on week-ends from Perrin AFB at Sherman, Texas some 250 miles to the north. We finally decided to get married before I left for my first fighter squadron assignment in Dayton, Ohio, February of '54. So in December '53, we tied the knot.

Like most young newly-wed couples, and in particular fighter pilots, we start having kids and living on peanuts which is about all a second lieutenant's salary allowed. Financial planning and budget control was not high on our priority list. We were happy living an Air Force life, being with Air Force people and couples our age who were all in the same boat. We weren't rich, far from it, but we were having a great time raising the kids, going to squadron parties and picnics and in general just having a great time. I was flying jet fighters, and the kind of flying we did in those years was probably the most fun than any of the others that followed. Flying two and three times a day at an hour and twenty minutes each was common practice. Flying time was plentiful and restrictions were not as tight as they would become in the years that followed.

After about 4 years in the fighter squadron and a General's Aide tour at

Wright-Patterson AFB, Dayton, Ohio, and Squadron Officer School under my belt, we were assigned to another F-86 fighter squadron in Morocco, then to an RF-101 (Tactical Reconnaissance role) squadron in France. We then returned to the states to an F-106 Air Defense Fighter squadron. I was having a ball staying in fighter squadrons and flying day after day since entering the Air Force. It had been 13 years of flying fighters as a company grade officer when I was finally promoted to Major and with that promotion came an assignment to the Air Force's Air Command and Staff College (ACSC) for nine months of professional military education. The school year (from September '65 to June '66) went fast. My next assignment was to Southeast Asia (SEA) in an F-105 with training for that role at McConnell AFB, Wichita, Kansas for about four months. Getting back to a fighter cockpit again is what I had hoped for. But this time, it was a combat fighter assignment and that seemed to be even better.

Over the past year ('65-'66) at the school, we had been kept up to date on the air war in Vietnam that was quickly developing, particularly the F-105's and the losses being sustained. In the fall of '65, I learned that one of my friends, Harry DeWitt, who was in an RF-101 Squadron with me in France, had been shot down in a F-105 in NVN. He had been injured during ejection and was in the Maxwell AFB (Montgomery, Alabama) hospital where I was attending ACSC.

As soon as I found out that Harry was in the hospital, I visited him. Harry had apparently taken a hit on one of his missions and made it to the Gulf of Tonkin coast before he was forced to eject over water. He told me he sustained a broken leg above the knee by the force of the ejection seat hitting him as he ejected. I was glad to see Harry, and we rehashed old times in the Recce business, but from the tales he told, I soon became aware of what was really happening in the air war, and in particular, the kind of missions the F-105's were being tasked to fly and where.

At that time, I did not have any idea that I would end up with an assignment in F-105's, but I was keenly aware that the F-105's were the ones carrying the load for the bombing of the north in Vietnam. I was surprised to learn also that F-105s were only being based in Thailand. This brought them closer to the northern targets and the Hanoi area. In fact, being based in Thailand meant that those planes were restricted from bombing targets in South Vietnam by some sort of U.S./Thai agreement. Supposedly, these aircraft were only carrying out interdiction missions, which would prevent supplies and troops from infiltrating to the South, but the Thai's did not want to be involved in allowing a guest nation to station their war making machines on their soil for the purpose of fighting the war in the South.

It wasn't until February, '66 that my ACSC class of about 800 Captains and Majors, received orders for our next assignments. By then, all of us knew that those of us who were rated pilots and had not had a remote tour within the past year or two (95 %) would probably get orders to combat flying duty. Since all of my flying, some 14 years and 3000 hours were in fighters, I fully expected a choice fighter assignment. I did not want a Forward Air Controller (FAC) assignment for sure. I was really looking forward to an F-105 assignment and that's what I received. I was happy as hell! Like a pig in mud. It sounded like I would really get my feet wet in a great combat role with an aircraft that was doing the bulk of the bombing up north, and that suited me fine.

Some others who drew an F-105 assignment were not very happy. There was a lot of talk by some about putting in their papers or trading assignments with other classmates who might want the F-105. Some were successful in trading assignments.

By now, the news media were carrying stories more frequently about the Vietnam conflict with increasing attention to the loss rate or stories about the types of aircraft being shot down and the Prisoner of War (POW) episodes with pictures of the downed aircraft and pilots. At that time, the bad publicity was not a factor for me. I felt that I had been trained all these years in fighters, and had a lot of experience. Now the time has come for the Air Force to call on me to do what I had been trained and had been paid for all those years. I felt I owed it to the country and the Air Force to salute smartly and do the best job I could, no matter what assignment it was.

I now began to focus my attention on learning everything I could about the role of the F-105 in NVN. The MIA/POW's were becoming more and more of a hot issue in this country. Pictures began to surface showing pilots being paraded through the streets of Hanoi, all bandaged up, with stories about their F-105's being shot down etc. It was beginning to get my attention.

By the time I got to McConnell AFB for F-105 training in August, the air war was heated up and the Air Force was heavily involved in bombing North Vietnam with the F-105 as the primary weapon.

My four months of F-105 training was to last through December '66, with the last two weeks at George AFB, California for gunnery with practice bomb training on the ranges that were located in that area. My orders were for me to leave Wichita, Kansas on January 11 to San Francisco, stay at Travis AFB, California, then depart from San Francisco to Clark AFB in the Philippines the next day for jungle survival school for about a week before proceeding to the 333 TFS at Takhli AB in Thailand.

December was a short month with very little time spent with my family since I left for my last two weeks of training at George AFB just before Christmas. I would only have the rest of December and the first 10 days in January left before leaving for Thailand. It was bitter cold those first two weeks in January in Wichita, and school for the kids had resumed after the holidays. I guess the hardest part for me was the night before and the very morning of my departure.

I was able to handle the good-byes to Diane (14) and Carol (12) fairly well as they left for high school that morning. They were older and they had friends which seemed to occupy them enough, so saying good-bye to Dad one more time was not a big deal for them. They were use to seeing me go away on TDYs enough and were accustom to it. They understood where and why I was leaving but I'm not sure they knew the risk involved in this trip.

My problem at the time was saying good bye to Randy, my 10 year old son. I'll never forget that morning in the kitchen, by the sliding glass patio door where Randy left to go to school. He was bundled up with a leather hat, with ear flaps down to keep his ears warm for his walk to school that morning.

This was a typical January day in Wichita, Kansas. Snow was on the ground and it was really cold outside. Randy looked bewildered as I sat there trying to say good bye and trying not to seem concerned. I don't know if he really knew what was going on. I had a hard time keeping my composure. I remember hugging him really hard, then saying good bye, as he turned, opened the patio door and left for school. That was probably the most difficult moment for me of all the good-byes.

I now had to turn my attention to my one year old, Mark, and Bettye, my wife. Bettye would accompany me to the airport with one of my classmates, Maj. Wray Lasswell and his wife. Mark would stay at home with a baby sitter. Saying good bye to Mark was a little easier than Randy because he was just a baby and it just seemed easier knowing he really didn't know what was going on. I said my good-byes to Mark with one last big hug and kiss, then left the house with Bettye and all my gear.

We drove to the Wichita Municipal airport for my flight to San Francisco. The departure at the plane was not a pleasant one for me. What else can I say! The whole morning was full of good bye's and very sad. I was anxious to get on with it, and complete my tour, despite the feeling that I may not make it back.

I was glad Wray Lasswell was on the airplane with me. Wray had been an instructor in the Air University's Squadron Officer School at Maxwell AFB, Alabama while I was attending the University's Air Command and Staff College. We both had been assigned to the same F-105 Replacement Training Unit (RTU) class at McConnell AFB. The Lasswell's rented a house across the street from us in Derby, Kansas so we became good friends during our four or five months of F-105 training. Our follow on orders had us leaving the same day for our SEA tour in Thailand. Being on the airplane together helped me take my mind off the family and I suspect this was also true for Wray. It turned out that another classmate and friend, Maj. Don Fryhauf was on the airplane with us. Don was also in our RTU class but both he and Wray were being assigned to the 388 TFW at Korat AB, Thailand.

Don was also a close friend. We had been athletes at the University of Iowa together and were both lettermen, but in different sports. Don played varsity football and I played varsity baseball and only freshman football. We were also both in the Air Force R.O.T.C. program, but Don was a year ahead of me. He was in the class of '51, and I was in the class of '52. During those years, I remember Don being one of Iowa's finest running halfbacks in '49 and '50. In fact he had been nominated for "Big Ten" All-American football honors by one of the national magazines. Although we were not close friends during our college days, I always had a lot of respect for his athletic ability. At Iowa, we traveled in different circles. Don was a local Iowa City boy and my home was in Chicago, Ill., but was on a baseball scholarship to Iowa as a pitcher. I had earned two letters, and during my junior year after I pitched a shutout against the University of Wisconsin in '51, I was offered a contract from the Boston Red Sox. I wanted to finish college with a degree and also qualify for pilot training through the Air Force R.O.T.C. program, so I decided to not sign a contract. The Korean war had started, and draft notices were being received by many of our college classmates but as long as you continued in an R.O.T.C. program, you were deferred. However, the R.O.T.C. program required a 4 year military commitment following graduation and an Air Force commission. I decided to stay in school.

I hadn't seen Don since he left the U. of Iowa in '51 until this assignment.

Don had not changed much, physically or personality. He was still as strong as a bull and it was apparent that he still kept himself in good physical condition.

All three of us stayed together throughout the trip to SEA, jungle survival school at Clark AFB, and on to Bangkok where we finally split company. I proceeded to Takhli Air Base and Wray and Don to Korat AB. All of us hoping to reach that Magic 100 missions. All three of us did.

I must say here that during the entire tour, except during the missions I flew, family was always on my mind. It's one of those things that keeps you going and seems to give you some extra incentive for survival and that extra bit of courage you need when the going really gets tough.

# Chapter Two
# Combat Indoctrination (First Mission)

Flying my first combat mission was an experience full of anxious anticipation and a real eye opener. The local area check-out at Takhli for a newly assigned pilot was his first combat mission. No local indoctrination flights as such, but rather the real thing. The luxury of training flights for any non combat sorties was out of the question and just not possible because of aircraft availability to meet the target tasking. Every sortie needed to be scheduled for a combat/bombing mission.

My first several days after arrival at Takhli were devoted to getting housed and drawing personal flying equipment that was unique to flying combat. A survival vest with all the various survival items neatly fitted into every nook and cranny available was issued; a .38 pistol with tracer ammunition and shoulder holster; survival flares; and plastic baby bottles to be used for carrying drinking water in case of a shoot down. One of the things learned from those who were shot down and rescued was that one became very thirsty following a shoot down and the desire for water was overwhelming. The shock of being shot down, in addition to all the sweating one did during the entire mission was enormous. The dehydration that took place in this very hot and humid climate was a tremendous drain on body fluids. In fact, all our F-105 cockpits at Takhli were equipped with water bottles fixed to the side of the ejection seat about shoulder level with a long plastic drinking tube to drink from while in flight. You had to remove your oxygen mask to use it, but it really helped to have some water during some of the three to four hour missions.

Incidentally, I was really surprised to find all the F-105s modified with ash trays for smoking in-flight. Although I was a pack a day smoker, I never smoked in flight. Many guys did, but you really had to be careful because of the oxygen being pumped in through the oxygen mask which really set you up for a self induced fire in the cockpit. This happened to one of our pilots and he got burned pretty bad before he was able to extinguish it.

Our "G" suits were also modified with extra pockets sewed onto the lower legs to hold additional signal flares or water bottles. The more flares and water you could carry, the better chance you had for survival and rescue.

Special combat jungle flying boots were also an additional issue item. They were black leather with a nylon web top from the ankle up with a thick grooved hard rubber type sole. The nylon top didn't give much ankle support needed for a parachute jump landing nor were they very fire resistant since they would tend to melt instead of burn. Hot melted nylon on your skin is not a pleasant thought. They were however, cooler and more comfortable than the all leather flying boots we wore in the states.

After drawing all our combat flying gear, we went through some "Theater" indoctrination briefings. These consisted of rules of engagement and restrictions, our air order of battle (AOB), North Vietnamese defenses and capabilities, our local rules, flying procedures, weapons used (types of bombs and fuses), lessons learned, and the all important rescue procedures (safe areas and escape and evasion procedures). It was like drinking out of a fire hose. At first, I expected the briefings to be like the same ole base indoctrination briefings back in the states, but very quickly, I began to realize this was more serious and I better pay attention to what the old heads were telling us. It began to sink in that this flying tour was more than just another peacetime flying assignment. We were talking about "real" bombs, enemy defenses, survival procedures, and pilots who were here yesterday but no longer with us today. A sense of realization set in. The real combat world is upon me. I was now part of that world and from now on, flying would somehow be different than any I'd experienced before in the past 15 years and some 3,000 hours of fighter time.

Now, with all that preparation to begin flying combat missions behind me, I couldn't wait to get my feet wet in this new world of combat flying. I was eager as hell and felt confident that I could handle any situation and contribute to the overall effort in the interdiction mission the F-105s had been given in North Vietnam. My attitude was, "send me in coach, I'm ready to go". This was probably the attitude most of the pilots had when they arrived. The new pilots were all primed and ready for that combat flying role they'd heard so much about. I was no exception, and I couldn't wait to get into route pack 6 to see the infamous "Thud Ridge" everyone talked about. The thrill of the thought excited me and every new pilot that arrived. As a new pilot in this F-105 combat role, you didn't feel that you were part of the experienced group of combat seasoned veterans unless you had been to pack 6 with a strike force. Their was no doubt that the ultimate combat experience was going to pack 6 on a JCS target. Later however, sometimes I would wish that I didn't have to make another trip to pack 6. The thrill was always there however, but it took on a different meaning as the enemy defenses increased in numbers and became more sophisticated.

I arrived at Takhli on January 31, and after about a week of getting settled and indoctrinated, I was scheduled for my first combat mission on February 6 to bomb some bridges in the Dong Hoi area. Dong Hoi was located in route pack 1 on the North Vietnam Gulf coast just north of the 17th parallel that divided the north from the south. Dong Hoi was noted for being well defended and had been credited with downing several aircraft during attacks in that area. For my first mission, I was scheduled with two experienced captains in a flight of 4. One flew lead, the other number three. Another new pilot like myself flew wing as number four.

The flight briefing covered everything the two old heads could think of with particular emphasis to how we'd handle anyone who might be shot down, the safe areas for ejection and rescue procedures, North Vietnamese defenses at Dong Hoi, specific flak sites that were reported to be active along with the personal experiences of the shooting they encountered the last time these two old heads had been there. As a result, I expected to see a lot of shooting at us over the target area Since I had never been shot at before, I really didn't know what it would look like or exactly what to expect.

Arriving at the aircraft for my first combat mission and preflighting it with 6/750 lb bombs hung on the multiple ejection rack (MER) with all the safety wires and red flags hanging off the bombs seemed unreal. There was a sense of realization that these were real bombs that are really going to destroy the hell out of whatever we drop them on. They were not at all like those small blue colored foot long training bombs we used back in the states for training. When we were training, no one was shooting at us, and we dropped one little blue bomblet at a time for scoring purposes. But now, I was amazed at how awesome that F-105 looked with the bombs and the 2/450 gal fuel tanks hanging on the wings of the aircraft. My thoughts were, this is for real, not training. We're really going out to destroy and/or kill people with these bombs along with that internal 20 MM gatling gun loaded with 1,000 rounds of real ammo stuffed in the nose of the F-105.

One of the things that really got my attention on this first mission that I'll never forget is when we arrived in the weapons arming area at the end of the runway just prior to takeoff.

We all started engines at the agreed start engine time as 4 F-105 start cartridges fired almost simultaneous adding those all to familiar loud explosions and black smoke to the already noisy flight line. After several minutes of pre-taxi checks in the chocks with the crew chief, we taxied out in formation order, 1,2,3,4, in a staggered fashion to avoid the jet fumes and foreign objects from being ingested into the engine intakes from the aircraft in front.

It was always hotter than blue blazes during taxi operation. Temperatures at Takhli would run in the hundreds with 90 to 100% humidity. By the time you climbed into the cockpit after preflighting the aircraft, you were completely soak and wet, like coming out of the shower with your clothes on. While taxiing with the canopy slightly cracked open and the oxygen mask on, perspiration would accumulate in the oxygen mask to the point where you had to unstrap it and shake the perspiration out or it would clog the valves. Most of the time, you just taxied with the mask hanging loose and just put up

*F 105 flight line starting their engines.*

with the jet fumes from the aircraft in front of you. Sweat would completely soak the foam rubber pads in the helmet also. The pads only lasted a few missions and then had to be changed because of the deterioration caused by the moisture. Once airborne however, the cockpit could be cooled down to a comfortable level with the air conditioning system. It was a relief to get airborne just to cool off.

We finally arrived in the arming area, which was an enlarged concrete area, at the end of the runway where the aircraft were finally armed up just before takeoff. A weapons arming/de-arming crew, and some maintenance crew chiefs would be standing by to pull all the safety pins on the weapons (bombs and missiles) and check the entire aircraft over for any fluid leaks, tire cuts and just general condition of the aircraft to ensure we'd be taking off with good aircraft. Sort of a "last chance" to detect anything wrong with the aircraft before you launched. Sometimes, tires could be cut or leaks develop while taxiing this fully loaded beast the fairly long distance from the parking ramp to the takeoff end of the runway.

Normally, we pulled into the arming area and lined up at sort of an angle with the nose of the aircraft facing out into the uninhabited area in case an ammo round or missile inadvertently fired off. Usually, the area looked busy as hell with as many as 8 aircraft in front of you being prepared for takeoff and crew chiefs running all around the aircraft, pulling red streamer pins from the bombs, missiles etc. As soon as you pulled into your slot, the canopy was raised and both hands had to come in view of the arming people as a safety precaution. This procedure prevented the pilot from fooling around with the weapon switches in the cockpit while they were underneath the aircraft inspecting and pulling the safety pins from the weapons.

As I pulled into my slot, I raised the canopy. I then raised my hands by resting my elbows on the canopy rail and burned the hell out of my elbows. You could have fried an egg on any part of the aircraft, it was so hot. I quickly removed my elbows from the canopy rail and just displayed my gloved hands on top of the glare shield so the crew chief could see them. Only then did the maintenance and arming personnel disappear under the aircraft to arm and check the aircraft over. Soon, they re-appeared holding a handful of red streamers and pins and gave me a thumbs up signal.

What happened next was totally unexpected. I had noticed earlier that there was this officer in a flying suit sort of standing in the background as all these other airmen were scurrying around doing their job. I thought he was probably one of the supervisors who was making sure everything went well. I also noticed that this officer had a black book in his hand and a colored, I think it was purple, scarf thing hanging around his neck over the collar of his flying suit. After the arming crew chief gave a thumbs up, this guy walked forward to the lead aircraft near the cockpit area and disappeared from my view. Suddenly, he reappeared and walked briskly over the left side of my aircraft, just under the cockpit, looked up at me, and put his hand up in front of his face, made the sign of the cross, reached up, and made the same sign as he touched the skin of the aircraft. I then realized that this was the Chaplain who was blessing each pilot and aircraft just before takeoff. I thought, "Jesus, we're being given our last rites". That got my attention, big time!

Again, the realization of what flying combat means came back to me. It seemed like I kept getting these messages about combat flying being hazardous to your health and down right dangerous. Like, It could get you killed! I could be shot down and this could not only be my first, but also my last mission. It really makes you think about reality. So for 100 missions, if I was lucky, the aircraft and I would be given the Chaplain's blessing each time before takeoff. Actually, once you got over the initial shock, and got use to it, it wasn't a bad idea. In fact, I kind of liked it. The funny thing about it was that this was one of the things that was never briefed to a new pilot prior to his first mission.

We finally got airborne and proceeded east to North Vietnam, the coast, and the target, Dong Hoi. Although no pre-strike refueling was planned, post strike refueling would be needed for the return to Takhli. After we crossed into Laos from Thailand, we armed up the bombs and gun and got ready to strike once we arrived in the target area. As we approached Dong Hoi, I could pick up the bay area, town, bridges, and prominent bomb pock marks where other aircraft had dropped their bombs all over the area.

The leader intentionally overflew the area about 2 or 3 miles to the north and proceeded out over the water to assess the target and any defenses that might become active. We were only about 6 or 7,000 feet, the weather was clear and visibility was unlimited. We did a 180 degree turn over the Gulf, from east to west, for a return to the Dong Hoi and final run on the target. As we approached the coast, inbound to the target, the leader reported that he detected some shooting from the ground and that he had the guns in sight. He informed us that he would go after the guns and for the rest of us to attack the bridge. I didn't see any shooting or guns and was disappointed that I could not pick up what the leader saw. In fact, I wasn't really convinced that anyone was shooting at us.

Later, I would find out that this was a typical attitude for the new guy who really hasn't experienced seeing the muzzle flashes of the guns, the flak puffs, or been hit, or seen someone hit. It's like the "I'm from Missouri, show me" attitude.

Lead rolled in for his strike on the gun site and I rolled in behind him for a drop on the bridge with 3 and 4 right behind me. We all dropped our bombs on one pass, came off the target, looked each other over to make sure we were clean and joined up in loose route formation. Lead decided to go back for another run using the 20 MM gun this time to give the target one more finishing touch. Again, Lead and 3 called that they were shooting at us again and of course I didn't see anything. We rolled in, strafed the bridge, got some good hits, rejoined, and left the area for the tanker to refuel prior to proceeding to Takhli.

All the way back, I couldn't believe how easy this was. It was fun. In fact, I felt disappointed somewhat, because I didn't see any shooting. I felt deprived of the experience of being shot at. I even wondered if the leader was just trying to impress us new guys by reporting that we were being shot at. I felt that if all the missions are like this, this tour will be a piece of cake.

One of the things you learn very quickly about the different types of weapons being shot at you from the ground is that the heavier millimeter antiaircraft guns (37MM, 57MM, 85MM, & 100MM) used almost exclusively for defenses of the pack 6 targets in North Vietnam actually detonated, exploded in mid-air if it didn't hit anything first. They were fused to detonate on time (seconds) or altitude. Large puffs are clearly visible when they explode. The 37MM explosions caused a white puff like a small white cloud. The 57MM explosions were a little larger and caused gray puffs, and the 85's, larger black puffs, with a fire ball sometimes visible when it's close enough to you to see. The shrapnel from the exploding round is what normally ripped into the aircraft if it wasn't a direct hit.

Smaller caliber weapons - or "small arms fire" - although also used in pack 6, were the primary weapons mostly used in the lower route packs. Very few heavy weapons were moved out of the Hanoi target areas. What this meant was that although you didn't encounter the heavy weapons in the lower packs, it was also more difficult to visually see if any weapons were being fired at you. The small arms were non-explosive ballistic rounds being thrown up at you. They did'nt explode, so you couldn't see the round unless tracers were used. They could be very lethal however, if you took a hit by one because most were "armor piercing rounds". These rounds could melt metal on contact and penetrate several layers of tough metal.

From personal experience, an armor piercing round could penetrate the aircraft's skin, main spar and instrument panel of an F-105 and still retain its shape as a recognizable bullet type ammo round. Most small arms weapons had tracers mixed into the clips so they could actually see where they were firing, visually. When tracers were used, it also helped us visually pick up the stream of rounds being fired at us and helped detect the location of the firing site.

During the debrief after this first mission with the intelligence folks, the flight lead and number 3 used the Recce photos of the target area and without hesitation, identified the location of the guns that had been firing at us. I was surprised that they were able to point out the precise location of these sites and other features which I was totally unaware of. For the first time, I began to believe that we were, in fact, being shot at but I just did'nt see it. Later, during the flight debriefing with all four of us, one of the points the leader made that made a lot of sense and proved to be good advice was, don't take for granted that no one is shooting at you just because you don't see it. Or said another way, always assume someone is shooting at you, even if you don't see it, because the odds are, someone is.

# Chapter Three
# We Bombed What? — My Third Mission

The intelligence debriefing folks were waiting for us when we returned from our lower route pack mission. A bridge across the small river in Laos that led to a friendly village had been bombed within the hour and had been reported to headquarters in Saigon. In addition, some bombs had strayed into the edge of the village killing some friendly Laotians. Reports were being received hours later that bombs were still going off because of the delayed fuses. Headquarters wanted to know who did it, and why.

It wasn't to difficult to narrow it down to just a few possible strikes that had been fragged ("fragmentation order" used to transmit the targets to the subordinate units) on targets in that area. Each target was identified by map longitude/latitude coordinates to the fighter wings to include time over targets (TOT), assigned refueling tankers, if required, with rendezvous points, bomb loads and fuses to be used which supposedly were tailored to take out that specific target. Only if the mission called for a route Recce of a particular road or railroad line might the actual target not be known before hand. In that case, you trolled that particular area looking for lucrative targets, trucks, rail cars, troops, etc.

The trouble with flying missions in Laos was that some areas in Laos were friendly and others were in North Vietnamese hands. In some cases, the "held" territory could shift from one day to the next. So it was very important to strike only those targets or Recce areas that were assigned or on the frag order. When missions were conducted in the lower route packs of North Vietnam, all targets were fair game but again, striking the assigned target was the number one priority.

However, rules for JCS targets in pack 6 were more specific. Only the fragged target could be hit or any defenses that were actually shooting at you. We were prohibited from bombing any other target in pack 6 but the one assigned. There were certain targets that were off limits during my tour such as active airfields and dams. Targets within a 10 mile circle around Hanoi were off limits at the time also. However, If we were attacked by Migs in pack 6 prior to the target, we were allowed to jettison the bombs in self defense, but if we arrived at the assigned target and found the weather bad, we were not suppose to drop on any other target. Supposedly, we were expected to fly back out of pack 6 with the bombs and either find another target in the lower route packs or jettison them in an uninhabited area or over water. To say the least, the rules of engagement in pack 6 were different than anywhere else and did not help the U.S. fighter pilots do their job.

This was my third mission along with Capt Gordon "Buz" Blackwood (later became my roommate and MIA/KIA). We would be flying with two experienced flight leads, Maj Mike T. as lead, and Capt "Buddy" Jones as element lead, Buz" number 4, and I was 2. The target was a road bridge over a small river (more like a stream) in Laos, close to the North Vietnamese border and east of Takhli. No pre or post strike refueling would be needed because of the relatively short distance from Takhli.

During the briefing for this mission at Wing Headquarters, we picked up our maps and flight plans which had been prepared the night before by other squadron pilots. The procedure of having the mission maps and flight plans prepared the day before by other pilots was normal for planning missions in our Wing. It was a good procedure and worked very well. After we picked up the mission maps, obtained our aircraft assignments, we normally spent some time in the Wing briefing room looking over the current Laotian Air Order of Battle maps for defenses in the general area of the target, along with the escape and evasion safe areas. Once we were satisfied that we had all the information we needed to conduct the mission, we proceeded to our squadron area building for a detailed flight briefing by the leader.

While we were looking at the target area maps in the Wing briefing room, I noticed how similar the terrain features at the target were to another bridge about 25 miles west of the target which we would pass over enroute to the assigned target. The similarity of the bridge over the small river, the village on the east side, and the small mountainous terrain around the area were almost identical. The difference for us would be that the target should be about 2 to 3 minutes more flying time along our planned flight path.

Having flown as a Tac Recce pilot in an RF-101 in Europe, I had gained a lot of respect for good dead reckoning/time distance type navigation, particularly at low altitudes. One of the things you pay attention to is terrain features. In addition, it was standard procedure to spend plenty of target study time before the flight to get a good mental picture of key turn points and especially terrain features around the target area for good identification. Of course, when you fly Recce missions, it's usually single ship, by yourself, so it's like you're the leader all the time for navigation purposes. In the fighter bomber business, you're usually in a flight of 4. If you're flying wing, it's more difficult to keep up with detailed navigation. But as the leader, although the navigating techniques are the same, maneuvering smoother for the benefit of the wingmen who are trying to stay with you at high airspeeds is an added responsibility.

We had determined during our flight planning phase that there were no known defenses around this bridge. It didn't seem like it was a high value type target. The weapons load called for each aircraft to carry 6/750 lb bombs with variable time (VT) fuses. This meant the bombs wouldn't necessarily detonate on impact but delay for whatever time was set in the fuses.

Takeoff was scheduled for early morning. It was still dark when we preflighted our aircraft and took off. Shortly after takeoff, number 3, "Buddy" Jones aborted with a mechanical problem, so Lead, number 4,", and I continued with the mission as a flight of 3. We climbed to about 13,000 feet as our cruise altitude to the target. We could see the sun starting to peak over the horizon during the climb, hitting us right in the eyes as we proceeded east toward the target. It looked like we'd hit our time-over-target (TOT) as scheduled and be waking a few Viet Cong up this morning nice and early.

A fully loaded F-105 with 6/750 lb bombs and two 450 gallon fuel tanks made maneuvering above 19,000 feet sloppy. In fact, when scheduled for pre-strike refueling, the highest refueling altitude we'd accept was 19,000'. Normally, 5 tankers (one for each flight of the 4/F-105s in the strike force) were scheduled to be staggered at 2,000' intervals, starting at odd altitudes from 17,000' down to 9,000' as the lowest. Occasionally, when we had to use 19,000', the flight that refueled on that tanker had to use the afterburner in the minimum range as the F-105 approached the full fuel mark. When this happened, the afterburner used almost as much fuel at that altitude as you were taking on. In addition, it was difficult to maintain a steady position on the boom while tapping the afterburner every so often to maintain a position on the tanker refueling boom.

The target was only about a 40 minute flight from Takhli. As we crossed the Thai-Laos border, Mike (lead), had the flight arm our bombs for the strike. This was normal procedure. He checked in with the airborne command, control and communication (ABCCC) aircraft (C-130) who tracked the flights entering and leaving the strike areas in Laos and North Vietnam. We identified ourselves, the target code name, TOT, fuel on board, ammo status, and estimated time remaining in the area.

The weather was clear and visibility was good with some early morning haze that restricted visibility somewhat at lower altitudes. Shortly after crossing the Laos border, Lead said he had the target in sight and said he'd circle it one time to look it over. As I checked my map and clock, it seemed that we shouldn't have been there yet based on time-distance and the Doppler navigation equipment (which was rarely accurate for pinpoint navigation). The terrain features looked similar, but I didn't remember passing the karst-like mountain that we should have passed that lay west of the target. I didn't think we had passed that check point yet, and we were earlier than our flight planned time in route called for. I was flying a loose route wing formation position trying to look at my map and flight plan card that was strapped on my knee pad. I just couldn't believe we were off our flight plan arrival time that much. This was only my third mission so I was reluctant to question the Leader. In retrospect, I should have said something to Lead about my doubts, but I didn't. Instead, I planned to talk to him about it in debriefing after we land to find out for myself why my calculations were screwed up because had I been leading, I would have missed finding this target and that concerned me.

We circled the bridge as lead talked to us about the bridge he had identified as the target and gave the flight the order and direction for the bomb run. He wanted us to roll in separately, one at a time. The other two flight members would hold high, watch for anyone shooting and get some bomb damage assessment before the next one would roll in.

We each rolled in separately, dropping our bombs. "Buz" Blackwood was last in and as he came off the target, we joined up for our return to Takhli. I joined on "Buz's" wing first and noticed he had two bombs hanging that did not release. I informed him about his hung bombs and told him to try and "pickle" them off since we were over an open area. "Buz" slowed down and tried to get rid of his bombs without any luck. I finally told him to be sure his bombs were armed properly on his arming panel and then just swipe (cycle) his bomb switch through all positions. Within a few seconds, both bombs came off the multiple ejection rack (MER) and dropped into the uninhabited jungle below. We then joined on our leader's wing and returned to Takhli with another mission under our belts. All the way back, I kept thinking about whether we hit the right target and if we did, how could I be that far off my calculations. How did I not recognize the terrain features in route and around the target? Things just did not seem right.

We made our way back to Takhli without any further conversation on the radio. As usual, after parking the aircraft, we were picked up by the personal equipment "bread truck" type vehicle that would take us to the parachute hooch where we would drop our parachutes off for inspection and then we'd continue on to Wing Headquarters for the mission intelligence debriefing. As soon as I met Mike T. in the truck, I asked him if he was sure we hit the right target. I tried to explain my navigation calculations to him which I thought put us short of the target and that I didn't think we had flown far enough east. I showed him my map and the two targets that looked alike and suggested that maybe we hit the one that was west of the assigned target. Mike assured me that we hit the right target and told me not to worry about it and that once I had a few more missions, I'd be more familiar with navigating in this area and target identification. I figured Mike was probably right and I decided not to bring it up again. After all, Mike had been one of our F-105 training instructors back at McConnell AFB, and had about 30 or 40 missions here already and had been designated as a flight lead. I didn't feel qualified to doubt him. He convinced me that we hit the right target.

In the debriefing room, all the flight members sat down at one of several tables that were set up with chairs for each member of the flight and the intelligence debriefer as usual. Each debriefing cubical had maps and charts of Laos and North Vietnam for reference. Air order of Battle maps were also available to revise any defenses we might have noticed that were new sightings and may not be annotated on the maps. The debriefer would have the target maps and any pre strike Recce photos that might help in assessing the battle damage when our strike photos were developed and analyzed.

All the F-105s had internal nose and tail photo cameras that would automatically run when you depressed the bomb release (Pickle) button on the cockpit control stick grip. Both nose and tail cameras became active and would run for a set length of time to take pictures of the bomb run from the nose and then the tail as you pulled off the target. I think there was about 75 feet of 9"X3" black and white film loaded in each camera. Usually, by the time we finished our debriefing, our bomb film would be ready to look at for a more accurate assessment of the target "battle damage". Photo intelligence interpreters (P.I.'s) were specialists who looked at the film and made the damage assessments. It occurred to me that our film would shed some light on whether the target we bombed was in fact the assigned target.

The debriefing started off with the obvious standard question of what target we were assigned to strike. But then, the questions began to focus on what target we bombed. The debriefer made his point clear at the beginning by telling us that they had a report that a friendly bridge had been bombed in Laos and that some bombs had strayed into the village just across the bridge and had done some damage to the village and killed some friendlies. Also, further reports would indicate that some bombs were still going off as though they had delayed fuses. Headquarters was making inquiries to all fighter units to see who may have been flying in that area with the ultimate purpose of determining who may have bombed this target. They already had visual reports from friendlies in the village which indicated that there were two or three aircraft involved. The records were indicating that some Navy or Marine aircraft may have made the strike. The problem was that this village was in the same area as our assigned target and the time of occurrence correlated with our strike time and we only had three aircraft in the flight.

From the conversations between the intelligence debriefer and our Leader, I became painfully aware that we were suspected as the flight they were focusing on. My thoughts immediately flashed back to my original feelings about striking the wrong target and Mike's disagreement. Since normally, the Leader handled the debriefing dialogue about the mission, I decided to support Mike in his assessment of where we bombed and not inject my thoughts about which target we hit. This thing was getting more and more serious and was no time for conjecture. I'd let Mike handle the debrief and let the photos and facts speak for themselves. Right or wrong, my input was not going to be volunteered.

I knew Mike was feeling uncomfortable about being questioned about the same thing we just discussed earlier, in private. I felt he was afraid I'd say something about my doubts. I made a decision to support Mike's position and stick to it. " Buz" sat in silence. He was aware of our conversation in the truck after being picked up from our aircraft and fully aware of my view before we found out that a wrong target had been struck. At that time, none of us really believed this thing was going to blow up into an international incident as it was beginning to appear. Our debriefing dragged on and on with questions and answers that seemed to point more and more toward our flight as the culprits. We looked at the camera film from each of the aircraft with the intelligence folks, and the P.I.s seemed to think the target we hit was not the same as the one we were assigned. Mike still insisted that we bombed the right target and "Buz" and I stood around in silence, other than to agree with Mike and lend support. Since I was on my third mission and "Buz" was on his first mission, there wasn't much credibility they attached to our views. The Leader was the key player and we were supporting him.

The debriefing ended with no in-house resolution as to whether we bombed the right target or not. As the three of us left Wing Headquarters and walked back to our squadron building which was about 100 yards down the street, there was silence. I finally broke the ice and told Mike that I thought this thing had not ended and that to forget what I had said to him in the truck, and that I'd support him in any further investigation that may take place. "Buz" chimed in and said he believed we hit the right target also and couldn't believe that we were being investigated with such enthusiasm over bombing a target in Laos. We couldn't believe headquarters would frag a target that close to a friendly village and not brief us about it during the mission pre-briefing. In any event, by the time we arrived at the squadron building we had all agreed to stick by the leader's decision. Mike was relieved and thanked us for supporting him during debriefing. Till this day, I really believe Mike believed sincerely that he bombed the right target.

As it turned out, a formal investigation ensued with a team of 2 or 3 members of which one was a F-105 pilot from Korat A.B. (our sister wing of F-105s at the 388 TFW). All of us were interviewed and questioned by the investigation team for the record. We all stuck by our belief that we had bombed the designated target. After the investigation was complete (within a couple of days), we were told that all the evidence indicates that our flight was the one that bombed the friendly bridge and damaged the friendly village killing several friendly Laotians. Only one other flight of fighters (Marine) were anywhere near the same area and their TOTs, bomb load, and target coordinates did not correlate with the incident in question.

As a result, Mike was taken off flight lead orders and restricted to flying wing position. About a month later, he was put back on flight lead status and successfully completed his 100 missions over NVN. "Buz" and I were allowed to continue flying as usual since we were given the benefit of the doubt as new guys who were just flying the lead's wing and following his decisions. I felt sorry for Mike.

Being taken off flight lead status was a terrific blow to his ego and somewhat of an embarrassment for him. I didn't think he deserved it. He was a good fighter pilot with a lot of experience. Despite this unfortunate experience, we remained good friends throughout the rest of his tour. I flew his wing several more times to pack 6 later in our tours without any reservations about Mike as flight lead. It was not encouraging for me to see what happened to Mike for just trying to do his job under some very confusing rules of engagement and self imposed restrictions when things don't go just right. If we were responsible for this incident, the thing that bothered us the most was being held responsible for killing the civilian Laotians not about bombing the wrong bridge. "War is Hell", as the saying goes, seemed to be pretty well thought out.

## Chapter Four
# Flying "Thuds" Into Route Package Six

Being assigned to an F-105 tour meant that you would be stationed in Thailand, either at Takhli or Korat AB. Furthermore, flying out of Thailand meant that any missions flown could not be against targets in South Vietnam, only the North. This was a U.S./Thailand agreement.

Early on in the conflict, from 1965 on, the F-105s had been given the task of interdicting the supply routes leading from the North to the South. Their primary mission was to carry out the bombing of these targets in North Vietnam as directed by the highest levels in the U.S. government. This required the F-105s to fly missions not only into the lower part of North Vietnam, but mostly into the Hanoi area, or "Pack Six". The pack 6 missions consisted of a strike force of five (5) flights of four (4) F-105s (20) scheduled to bomb targets in the Hanoi area, every day, twice a day. They were called "White Knucklers" for obvious reasons.

It was thought by some that the bombing of these targets in Route Package six was the key to bringing Hanoi to their knees and a final U.S. victory. It probably was, but the restrictive bombing policies by our government seemed to lack the resolve to allow the Air Forces to properly prosecute the bombing effectively to force North Vietnam to settle the conflict in our favor.

To put things into perspective, the war in Vietnam was divided into two distinctly different wars, the war in South Vietnam, and the one being fought in North Vietnam by the U.S. Air Forces. While the war in the south involved both ground and air forces, the war up north was strictly one of interdiction, fought by air forces of the three services, Air Force, Navy and some Marine. The 17th parallel divided the North from the South. The North was divided into 6 packages. Pack 6, as it was called, was the portion which included the area north of the Red River. Furthermore, pack 6 was divided into two sections, 6A and 6B. The 6A target area was assigned to the USAF and 6B to the Navy/Marines. The Lower route packs (1 thru 5), as they were referred to, were also divided up in responsibility between the Air Force and Navy.

When I arrived in Thailand, the squadron Commander's (Lt/Col Danny Salmon) "In-Brief" to me was that "Your in the Big Leagues now. The F-105s are the only Air Force units carrying the war to Pack Six and Hanoi. We're doing the majority of the bombing in North Vietnam. This is really the Big Leagues".

He was right, but I did not understand what he really meant. I thought he was just pumping me up as would be expected from a Squadron Commander (C.O.) briefing one of his new pilots. Little did I know how right Col Salmon was and how really "Big League" it was.

While I was at Takhli, an incident occurred which demonstrated what flying "Thuds" into Route Pack 6 was all about. We knew that the restrictions placed on us prevented us from bringing the war to a close. We didn't really care, because we knew what we were there for. We knew we were flying missions against the toughest defenses, especially in pack six.

The incident involved an F-105 "Force" (5 flights of 4 F-105s and a flight of 4 F-4 Mig Cap) out of Takhli against a "Joint Chiefs of Staff" (JCS) target in pack 6. I happened to be in the last flight of the 5 flights of 4 thuds. We took off in the early morning dark for a strike at first light in the target area. We had rendezvoused with five KC-135 tankers in Laos for refueling, just north of Udorn Air Base, Thailand. Each flight of 4 F-105's had its own tanker as they carried us north to the "tanker drop off point" which was suppose to be about 1900 North latitude in northern Laos.

The force was proceeding north down the track with each member of each flight cycling on and off the tanker, topping off our fuel so we would have a full load at tanker drop off point. We needed all the fuel the Thud could carry.

Normally, Lead and 2 were on one wing of the tanker and 3 & 4 were on the other wing, as we alternated taking on fuel. Usually in a 1,3,2,4 order so the one coming off the tanker would move back to his original position on the opposite side from the one going on the tanker. The procedure worked fine and it kept the refueling sequence moving quickly and safe. Many times, however, and mostly as we got close to the drop off point, things started to speed up as each tried to get topped off, down to the last second and drop of fuel.

*Flight of F-105Ds loaded with bombs refueling on KC-135 on way to target in NVN. Typical F-105 loose fingertip formation on tanker for refueling. Two on each wing, rotating in-turn for refueling along the refueling track until tanker drop off point around the 19th parallel in Laos.*

**THE THUD IS NO DUD**
It's the fighter-bomber
with the powerhouse punch

*From "The Airman" magazine — F-105D refueling on a KC-135 tanker boom on the way to NVN target. Note fueling streaming from the 450 gal external fuel tanks. This starts to happen when the F-105 is about full of gas. The outboard wing stations have ECM pods attached.*

Usually the indication that the F-105 was full of fuel while refueling on the tanker was the spraying of fuel from the tanker boom at the connection with the F-105. This meant that the F-105 was about full of fuel and disconnect was imminent.

So sometimes, when you saw fuel spraying out of the nozzle connection, the next guy on the tanker would fudge by dropping down and back to be in a position along side the disengaging fighter on the tanker to expedite his refueling. Bearing in mind that this occurred while the fighter was still on the tanker boom and before a disconnect was initiated. This was not normal procedure but most guys did it, including me. The risk was that if the guy coming off the boom broke off in the wrong direction, he'd run into you. It was a set up for a mid air. This is what happened to two of the F-105's in the flight in front of us on this mission.

Several miles and a couple of minutes before our tanker drop off point, there appeared a spectacular ball of flame, a tremendous explosion with a huge fire ball in front of us and slightly above our altitude. Pieces of airplane were falling out of the sky! There was a frantic call that sounded in my helmet's headset.

"We've had a mid-air". Then, "Mayday, Mayday, Mayday".

Beepers started to go off on the UHF "Guard" frequency. Chunks of burning aircraft were falling down in front of us. A chute came out of nowhere.

The leader of that flight called the force lead and told him that his number 2 and 3 had a mid air and that a chute was in sight. The Force Lead very calmly said, "Get a fix on his position and have the airborne spare fill in." He then called "Crown" (the rescue coordinator) to launch the rescue aircraft for recovering the pilot, and then added that we'd be back for assistance if needed when we return on egress.

Crown responded that rescue would be on the way. There was silence!. A few seconds later, we were at the drop off point and the force Lead called for "drop off". We proceeded to the target as usual, as if nothing had happened. It seemed Routine.

I might add that one of the pilots did survive and I don't know if he returned to finish his tour. He was lucky! The other pilot didn't make it!

The significance of this episode is that the mission came first and everyone knew it. Taking a strike force to pack 6 meant split second timing in order to rendezvous with tankers and Mig Cap. We had to arrive over the target (TOT) at the precise time to take advantage of the ECM laid down by the RB-66 ECM (electronic countermeasure) aircraft. Time over target (TOT's), and meeting them, helped avoid congestion from the other strike forces (Korat F-105s and the Navy strike aircraft) ingressing and egressing pack 6. Pack 6 targets were confined to a relatively small area. There was a lot of activity that transpired in a short period of time and very small airspace.

This was only one of many episodes that reflected the professional attitude of those pilots who flew the "Thud" in Vietnam to pack 6. We knew we had to press on if at all possible, without delay. It was not always easy to make quick decisions, but sometimes they had to be made for the success of the mission, and some were not always pleasant ones. It was indeed "Big League".

# Chapter Five
# *Strike Force/Flight Lead*

Whether you're the Strike Force Commander leading a formation of 5 flights of 4 F-105s into route pack 6 or leading a flight of 4 into the lower route packs, the flight lead's decisions could make or break the mission. A bad decision could result in putting the entire force in jeopardy for one reason or another. Since the primary mission for the strike force was to destroy the selected target, it was extremely important that the leader get the entire force into a position from which all flights could initiate a successful bomb run attack while at the same time minimize the time over target where the AAA flak was the heaviest. When attacking targets in strike force formation, the importance of initiating the attack on the first approach in route pack 6 was an absolute must. Circling the target was a no-no since it always "hung out" each succeeding flight in the string like sitting ducks in a shooting gallery. Once over the target, we were in a very vulnerable position, heavily loaded with bombs, slower than we wanted to be, and high enough to be easy targets for AAA and SAMs.

One of the many problems for a flight lead was finding the target far enough in advance to initiate the attack for a successful run without jeopardizing the rest of the flights in the force trailing behind. One of the causes seemed to stem from the obvious fact that there were no navigational aids in North Vietnam available for use to locate the target for the kind of bombing attack maneuver we used. Marginal VFR conditions with low clouds and often poor visibility in the target area usually contributed to the complicated task the flight leads had in visually locating the target early.

Even when the weather was not a factor, a lot depended on the amount of preflight preparation or "target study time" done by the flight lead and the flight lead's ability to use good dead-reckon navigation techniques. This meant accurate, smooth maneuvering based on time/distance and his ability to visually read terrain features. These were the only navigation techniques available to visually locate planned check points for arrival at the proper location for the successful bomb run to the target on the first approach. Timing and positioning were two key elements for success.

Most of the time, there was insufficient fuel for a second run at the target once the force arrived over the target. Initiating the attack on the first approach, was the most important element for the survival of the strike force.

Familiarity with the terrain features in pack 6 through repeated visits was probably the most helpful for anyone leading the strike force. Usually, the most experienced pilots who had been noted for making good decisions and who had been to pack 6 many times as flight leaders were chosen to lead the force. Therefore, not always were the Strike Force Commanders the most senior ranking pilots. This was rarely challenged by any senior ranking pilots relegated to following a more junior ranking flight lead. The policy was unanimously accepted and proven to be sound. In combat, when survival is at stake, common sense and good judgment usually prevails over any desire to exercise rank privileges.

Because of the tremendous responsibility laid on the Strike Force Commander, some were not eager to accept that responsibility. Others, wanted it even though they had not gained the necessary experience in pack 6 nor been ready for leading a force for one reason or another.

Two missions that I remember well illustrate some of the problems that can occur and the importance of having a well qualified Strike Force Commander in pack 6.

On my 81st mission, 20 July, 1967, the target was a new airfield being constructed outside the village of Yen Bai, just across the Red River, west-northwest of Hanoi in Route pack 6. The Force Commander on this mission was one of the Squadron Commanders in the Wing. We had gone through F-105 training together in the same class at McConnell AFB. I was flight lead of the last flight of 4 in a strike force.

*Surface-to-Air Missile (SAM).*

During this time frame, North Vietnam's active airfields were restricted from being attacked by our own (Washington) rules of engagement. However, although active airfields were off limits as targets, any new airfields being constructed were not. The aerial photos we had of the Yen Bai airfield construction showed a clearing for the runway along with some partially constructed buildings and a large area on one side of the field with a large quantity of 50 gallon fuel/oil drums. Our task was to crater the runway and destroy the petroleum area. Each of the four flights had one of these as a specific target area to bomb.

Although Yen Bai was not deep into pack 6, the area was loaded with AAA sites to protect the SAM site that was located there. The Yen Bai SAM site was noted for its activity and one that had been credited with sev-

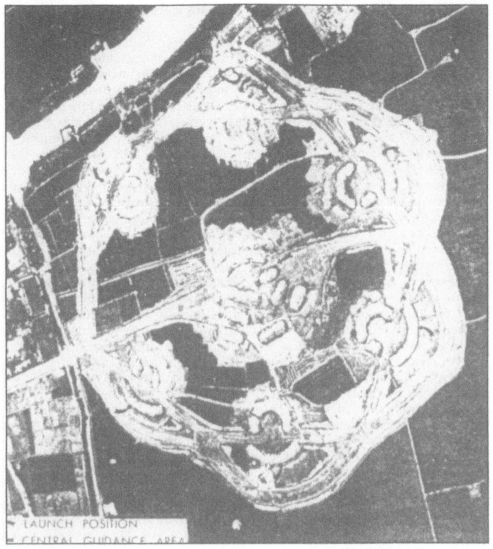

LAUNCH POSITION
CENTRAL GUIDANCE AREA

*Surface-to-Air Missile (SAM) Launch Site.*

eral American aircraft kills. Our normal ingress to other targets in pack 6 was always planned to avoid a 17 mile radius of an active SAM site if possible. Intelligence sources and our experience with SAM engagements indicated that that was their lethal range for accurate SAM guidance. Sometimes, our planned ingress and egress routes to targets could not avoid being within range of several SAM sites at the same time but "those were the breaks".

For this mission, the planned ingress route led us right into the Yen Bai SAM site range. We would penetrate pack 6 from the top of the karst mountains to the south of the target, drop down to the flat lands for a short period and then climb to about 12,000 feet in the pop-up maneuver as we crossed the Red River near Yen Bai. From the edge of the mountainous terrain, Yen-

Bai and the target area should be visible, with sufficient time to establish a good roll-in point for the dive bomb run.

Needless to say, climbing to those altitudes over the target was hazardous when SAM sites and radar tracking AAA were part of the defenses. Our most vulnerable time would be during the so called "Pop-Up" maneuver as we left the ingressing low altitude that helped mask our position from their radar and start climbing for the dive bomb roll-in altitude over the target. During that period, we'd be committed to maneuvering for a good bomb run and consequently have to ignore any flak or SAM activity. Total concentration would be fixed on maneuvering for the bomb run once the target was in sight.

Since I had been a Tac-Recce, RF-101 pilot in Europe some years earlier, I had some excellent low-level, dead-reckoning, time-distance navigation training. I never forgot the value of target study time during preflight planning, locating good recognizable terrain features on maps and target photos. Tac Recce pilots were probably the best trained pilots in the Air Force in low-level navigation and dead-reckoning techniques. They were trained to find the target on the first pass to take a single snapshot of the target at close to super-sonic speeds, on the deck. It took excellent training and a lot of experience before you felt qualified to do that sort of thing on the first pass.

I felt the low-level navigation training I had during that Recce tour adequately prepared me for the sort of flying we were doing in a combat role as fighter bombers. I always felt fortunate to have had this Recce experience.

No matter who was leading the force, I always made a point of studying the target area in detail for check points, key terrain features that would help identify the target early. As one of the flight leads in the force, I always thought it was a good idea to prepare myself as though I was leading the force. Aborts by the Force Commander were not unusual nor were shoot downs of the leader. Even though the Deputy Force lead (the Force Commander's element lead, number 3) was the next in line to take over leading the force, you never knew how much assistance either one may need as the mission unfolded in the maze of unforeseeable events.

Our mission briefing, take-off, rendezvous with tankers in northern Thailand (Green Anchor), and ingress into North Vietnam all progressed routinely. After drop off from the tankers and as we crossed the Black River in North Vietnam, on course, the F-105 weasel flight that was in front of the force by several minutes, began to report SAM warnings and Radar Control AAA signals to the rest of the flights. This meant we were on their radar scopes and an indication that they were getting ready for our arrival once we got in SAM and AAA range. The Yen Bai SAM site was reported active during our mission brief so it was no surprise that we'd be hearing from them. As we approached the Red River, my RHAW gear started to act up with sporadic aural and video signals. I decided to leave it on since the signals I was receiving seemed to correlate with what the Weasel flight was reporting.

We were rapidly approaching the end of the mountainous (Karst) terrain just south of the Red River and the Force lead started to descend. He called for afterburners (A/B) to accelerate in preparation for the final run to the target, 'Pop-up" maneuver, and roll in for the bomb run. We lit our A/Bs to stay in formation as a force, maneuvering to maintain the proper in-trail separation between flights to prevent bunching up during the final dive bomb run on the target.

Our speed increased rapidly from the additional thrust and descent as we slowly started down from the mountains to the flat area. We'd only be down in the flats for a short period before starting the pop-up maneuver for the Yen Bai airfield just across the Red River. It would give us that additional protection of speed and concealment at low altitude for as long as possible before climbing to the higher, more vulnerable altitude the enemy radar needed for good tracking.

It was relatively clear and visibility was unlimited. One of those unusual days in pack 6. As we approached the Red River, I could see the Yen Bai airfield about 10 o'clock, clearly identified. Off to the right, about 2 o'clock, I could see the Yen-Bai SAM sight. AAA (Flak), started to appear in front of us. White puffs (37MM) and barrages of gray (57MM) were bursting around the lead flight as he started to cross the Red. Someone made a call on UHF frequency to say "they're starting to shoot". It was obvious to all the flights, but it always seems that there is a compelling feeling to make the call anyway. The sky began to look like a cloud deck had instantly set in over the target and appeared to follow each flight as they came in range of the AAA.

The force lead had started his pop-up, climbing right into the more intense 57MM barrage. The number 2 and 3 flights in front of me started their climb, following the force lead as we crossed the Red River. As I looked ahead at the lead flight, I noticed that he was still climbing and making a shallow left turn, in sort of a circling maneuver. I wondered why he had not rolled in for the bomb run since it looked like he was in a good position to roll in on the target.

I glanced at my altimeter and I was surprised to see it passing 12,000 feet and we were still climbing. The leader and other two flights in front of me were much higher and I became concerned since we would soon be reaching a dangerously low airspeed with a full load of bombs. The control stick was beginning to feel sluggish and mushy. SAM activity was picking up and the flak was becoming thicker and more accurate. The guns were having a lot of time to home in on us at this altitude and slow airspeed. They were having great target practice as we were being "hung-out" slowly climbing and circling.

For the life of me, I could not figure out what the lead flight was waiting for. At 15,000 feet, I'd had it! I called the leader and asked if he had the target in sight. He only replied that he did, but he still gave no indication that he was rolling in or what his problem was. He just kept climbing in a slight left turn, circling the target.

I was in perfect position for a roll-in to the bomb run so I called the leader and told him I was rolling in with my flight. I didn't wait for an answer or approval. I knew the rest of my flight was getting nervous about being hung out like this and as I looked to my right at number 2, 3, and 4, in echelon, I could see that number 4 was having problems staying with us at this mushy airspeed and altitude.

I immediately initiated the roll in for the bomb run, rolled inverted, yanked the nose through toward the target to establish a good dive angle, then rolled back. The airspeed increased rapidly with the afterburner cooking. I could see the AAA guns lighting up, sort of twinkling in a ringed circle from two different sites on the airfield. I realized then that we were not only taking flak from the sites at Yen Bai from the east but also from some new sites on the airfield. Since the lead flight was the flak suppression flight, and they had not rolled in yet, the flak sites were having a free ride. I stayed in the dive bomb run longer than normal trying to eat up the altitude we'd gained so I had a lot of time to get the pipper on target (middle of the runway). I pickled the bombs at the planned altitude and broke off hard to get ready for the rejoin and egress with the rest of my flight.

As I looked back to see how the rest of my flight was doing and how well my bombs did, I finally saw the lead flight start their bomb run. They must have been at least 20,000 feet when they started. The other two flights behind the force lead were hard to pick up because of their altitude and all the flak puffs surrounding them. They were being eaten alive by AAA.

About that time, the weasel flight called a SAM launch and I immediately looked toward the Yen Bai SAM site and saw a cloud of smoke or dust coming from the site area. A SAM was being launched but it was hard to tell where it would be headed. It finally got airborne and quickly accelerated. As I jinked back away from the launch site to prevent turning any further back to the target area, I lost sight of the SAM for awhile until I reversed my turn. I was concerned that the SAM may be launched against our flight so I needed to pick it back up visually. I finally saw it heading west behind us on its way toward the flights in the bomb run over the target. The SAM did not appear to be tracking our flight, but I knew the other flights had to be the target and hoped they had the SAM in sight.

Usually SAMs are launched in multiples of three so I looked back toward Yen Bai for the other two, sure enough, there were the other two which had just been launched. They appeared to be heading in the same direction as the first one. As I looked back at the target area, there was tremendous cloud of dust being thrown up along with black smoke and fire coming from the oil drums which apparently had been hit by one of the flights. The last flight was in the bomb run and one flight was just coming off the target but someone was going to have their hands full evading the SAMs that were heading their way. Within only a minute, the SAM episode was over. The SAMs continued skyward passing through the flights over the target. They continued out of sight without exploding. Once they passed the rest of the force, I turned my attention to getting my flight joined up for the egress, return to the post-strike tanker rendezvous and Takhli where we'd debrief the mission and try to find out why we got hung-out over the target.

The debriefing back at Wing intelligence was full of disgruntled pilots with not to many good words for how the mission was conducted to say the least. The Force Commander didn't really have any good reasons for hanging the force out other than not being in a good roll-in position. He was looking for the flak sites that were shooting and was having problems trying to decide which one to roll in on. Apparently, he didn't understand that he was putting the other 3 flights in a very vulnerable position by hanging us out as sitting ducks, absorbing all that flak his flight was suppose to be suppressing, all the while we're running out of valuable airspeed and maneuvering room. We were all lucky that day. Even though a few guys took some hits and damage from the flak, no one was shot down.

After the debriefing, many of the pilots who flew that mission openly expressed their apprehensions about flying in a force again that was led by that particular Force lead.

This mission only re-emphasized the importance of the valuable lessons we had already learned earlier about how important the Force Lead is. His ability to put the rest of the force in a good position for a desired dive angle once over the target was the key to success and minimizing losses. Once it's realized the approach to the bomb run is less than desirable you're stuck with it. Trying to salvage a poor set up by circling for a better dive angle at the expense of the rest of the force is a poor choice of options. Again, one of the most important lessons learned from flying in a force to pack 6 was "don't circle the target even if it's a poor set up on the first approach. Take what you have, make the best of it, or let the other flights in first if they're in a better position, but don't hang the force out like sitting ducks".

Maj. Ralph Kitchens demonstrated that last point as Force Lead during one of our pack 6 missions.

Ralph and I shared living quarters in a 2 man trailer during the later part of my tour and we became the best of friends, sharing our thoughts and views on everything. I had the greatest respect for him both as a personal friend and fighter pilot. We were contemporaries with the same date of rank as Majors, had entered the Air Force about the same time and had relatively the same amount of fighter flying experience. Ralph had spent most of his flying with Tactical Air Command (TAC) while mine had been mostly in Air Defense and TAC Recce.

Ralph arrived at Takhli and was assigned to the same squadron (333 TFS) with me the same day. He had been flying F-105's in Europe so he had the benefit of much more experience in the F-105 fighter bomber role unlike most of us who acquired our F-105 experience at a 4 month Replacement Training Unit (RTU). Ralph was a huge, six foot, barrel chested guy who you would not want to tangle with. His reputation as one of the best pilots in the wing was well known by all who had been stationed with him in Europe and by those

*Takhli Officers (Pilots) living quarters in trailers. Located adjacent to O'Club. Trailer divided in half for 2 pilots sharing one bathroom. Considered best living quarters at Takhli.*

who had the pleasure to fly with him in combat, as a wingman or leader. He became one of the Force Commander candidates very quickly after his first few trips to pack 6. I always felt comfortable when Ralph was a member of the force, particularly when he was the Force commander or in the same flight with me. One of the things most guys worried about was whether they could count on a flight member to do all they could to get you out if you went down. That is, "will this guy put his life on the line for me if and when the time comes?" Ralph was that kind of guy. In fact, he had proven it on several occasions during some rescaps and on one occasion by taking on some Migs to protect me on my first pack 6 mission.

Our target on this particular mission was the Thai Nguyen Ammo storage facility just east of the steel mill and rail yard near the Thai Nguyen village in pack 6. The target was just east of Thud Ridge about 20 miles. From the IP (the highest point on Thud Ridge, 5,223'), a left turn to an easterly heading and after about 2 minutes, at our normal planned speed of 540 Kts, we would be at the target.

Ralph was leading the force of 4 bomb flights, a weasel flight of 4, and the flight of 4 F-4 Mig Cap aircraft. I was leading the second bomb flight just behind Ralph's. Ralph's flight was the flak suppression flight, carrying Cluster Bomb Unit (CBUs) bombs. Each aircraft in our flight carried the usual 6/750 lb bomb load.

Ralph and I had over 80 missions under our belt and had been to Thai Nguyen several times to bomb the steel mill, rail yard, and Army barracks, so this new target, the Ammo storage facility should not be hard to find. We had good Recce photos to look at and the intelligence folks briefed us on the specific area and buildings the frag order wanted destroyed. They pointed out some significant terrain features in and around the area and active AAA sites we could expect to be shooting at us over the target. Several SAM sites were active within the lethal range on ingress, over the target and on egress.

Thai Nguyen was noted for its heavy defenses. The first few attacks on the steel mill and huge rail yard a couple of months earlier in '67 cost us dearly in several F-105s being shot down during these attacks. The Thai Nguyen complex was surrounded with lucrative targets. The North Vietnamese knew it and so did we. As a result, AAA sites were strategically located all over the area along with a few SAM sites. The photos we reviewed in our briefing before the mission showed the enormous damage to the steel mill and rail yard. The whole area was pock marked with huge bomb craters everywhere. The steel mill buildings were just shells of twisted concrete and steel. The railroad yard looked like it was rendered completely unusable with the railroad tracks twisted and broken extending from one end of the yard to the other. Still, occasionally the steel mill and rail yard would be fragged as targets. However, now we were concentrating on the ammo storage area located next to the steel mill/rail yard area.

As we crossed the Red River at our check point (prominent bend in the river) west of Yen Bai, Ralph put the force in afterburner to accelerate to our 540 Kts planned speed. From here on in, we'd be more precise to establish our in-trail spacing, staying as low as we could in order to avoid the SAM and radar detection system used to control AAA as well as Migs that might be trolling the area looking for us.

In a matter of just a couple minutes, we arrived at another check point, a "Y" in a small river, just west of Thud Ridge where we swung to the southeast which would now lead us to the northwest end of the ridge and the final IP, the highest point on Thud Ridge. With the force intact and really humming along, bombs were banging together on the Multiple Ejection Rack (MER) and the turbulence and bumping made flying formation for the wingmen difficult, especially for number four. The Weasels, who were out in front of the force, were already in the target area and starting to troll for SAM activity, reporting some SAM threat warnings to the force but no firings had occurred. Radar controlled AAA was also being reported at Thai Nguyen which meant we could expect some accurate flak over the target. I hoped they thought we were after the steel mill or rail yard and by some chance we might surprise them as we continued past both on our way to the ammo storage area.

As we completed our right turn to an southeasterly heading and staying on the south side of Thud Ridge, the peak was clearly visible. The weather was clear and visibility at the target area was unlimited. All we had to do was acquire the ammo storage facility amongst the other buildings in the area and that didn't look like it was going to be a problem.

Ralph's flight arrived at the Ridge turnpoint and started his left turn to the east toward Thai Nguyen for the final leg to the target. As soon as my flight completed the in trail turn behind Ralph's flight, I put the flight in echelon formation to the right for our left roll in to the target. After about a minute, I could now see what looked like the terrain features at the Ammo storage site that identified it from the other buildings in the same area. Ralph started to pick up some flak, both 37 and 57 (white and gray puffs) but he hadn't started to climb for the pop-up maneuver. Since I was only about a mile in trail with Ralph's flight, it seemed as though he should have started to maneuver for the bomb run if he had the target in sight.

I was approaching what I thought was my pop-up start point for a good roll in, but Ralph was still proceeding straight and level, almost abeam the target. At this point, I was convinced Ralph didn't have the target in sight, so on UHF, I asked Ralph if he had the target in sight. He quickly replied that he didn't and that if I did, to roll in first. I rogered his call, told him I had the target in sight and started my pull up for the roll in. For me, the ammo storage site was pinpointed by a small lake or pond of water which I made a note of on the target photos during briefing. However, the lake wasn't very prominent on any of the maps. Once I had the water in sight, the target had to be a slight distance to the north. Only then was I able to distinguish the ammo site as the target from the other buildings in and around the same area.

Ralph didn't stand on ceremony. He made the decision quickly because he knew there could be no delay with three other flights behind him and flak being thrown up at an increasing rate.

I pulled our flight up and we became engulfed in a mass of gray and black flak. I took one look to my right to see if the rest of the flight was still intact and ready to roll in. Four was trailing slightly, but was still hanging in there. I arrived at the right point for a good steep dive angle, rolled in, established a good angle, jockeyed slightly to get my pipper on the target and pickled my bombs. Since we were the first flight in, and no flak suppression in front of us, we were really catching hell from several flak sites. All the way down the chute, I continued to see flak going off below me and all around. How I managed to get through it all without taking a hit, I'll never know. My flight came off the target in tact and we began joining up as I headed back toward Thud Ridge for egress.

As was the usual procedure, when each member joined up, we looked each other over for any hung bombs and hits. As my number two wingman joined on me, he called to say I looked clean but as I looked him over he was clean but had fuel spraying from the top of his fuselage, about half way between the cockpit and the vertical stabilizer.

I called him and advised that he may have taken a hit because he had fuel siphoning from the top of his fuselage. He replied that he felt a slight "thunk" during the bomb run but didn't think much of it at the time.

If you've never seen an aircraft siphoning fuel, especially traveling at high speeds, it looks like hell. It looks like it's loosing gobs of fuel sometimes, when in fact, it's really not loosing a lot. It's hard to tell how much unless you monitor your fuel gages and then by timing the loss over several minutes, determine a rough estimate of the loss rate. The problem with loosing fuel as a result of a an unknown piece of flying metal ripping a hole into your fuel tank is that you really don't know what other damage it may have done nor where and how much of the fuel may be flowing into other interior parts of the aircraft. In the case of the F-105, the fuselage portion of the aircraft is all fuel tanks and they surround the engine as well. There are no wing fuel tanks. The wing area is dry which I always thought was a good idea when you're flying in combat. For the most part, there was some comfort in knowing that any hits we took in the wing area would not cause the loss of fuel or worse, a fire or explosion.

On our way to the tanker, I kept a check on number two's fuel state against mine and it seemed as though at the rate he was losing fuel, we shouldn't have a problem reaching the tankers. To be on the save side, I called the rescue coordinator, "Crown", and asked them to move the tankers further north and alert the rescue force in case we needed them for one of our F-105's that had some battle damage and was loosing fuel. By the time we rendezvoused with the tankers for refueling, his loss rate had slowly increased. Normally, when we refueled on the way out (post-strike refuel), we told the tanker how much fuel we each needed for recovery back home. I put number two on the tanker first and was surprised that he only asked for the normal amount of fuel, about 4,000 lbs. I called two and told him to get a full load since it looked like he was beginning to lose more fuel as time went on. He reluctantly agreed and took on the extra load.

Takhli was about another 40 minutes flying time and by the time we arrived, two had lost almost all his fuel, and he was beginning to sweat not having enough to make it back to the base. As it turned out, he landed and parked with about 500 lbs showing on the fuel gage. When we met in the Van that took us from our aircraft to the debriefing building, he told me how glad he was that I talked him into taking on a full load of fuel at the tanker.

# Chapter Six
# *Welcome to Pack Six*
## *26 April, '67, Mission #31*
## *Hanoi Thermal Power Plant (10 Mi. North of Hanoi)*

Since my arrival to the 333 rd TFS at Takhli, the last day of January 1967, I had only flown 6 missions by the end of February. By the end of March, I'd accumulated only 19. Weather in pack 6 had been bad, with low ceilings, fog and haze making the visibility at low altitude usually less than a mile. This caused many of the pack 6 missions to be canceled until around the middle of April. Once I had my 10 lower route pack missions, I was eligible for pack 6. Although I had been scheduled on several, it seemed they were either canceled for alternate lower route pack missions before takeoff or diverted in route. When the time came on 26 April, I felt I was really ready. I had completed 30 missions and was really chomping at the bit to get my feet wet in pack 6.

The 31st (1st 6 pack mission) was a very exciting but humbling mission. This target was the Hanoi power plant, about 10 miles north of Hanoi. I saw my friend, Maj Dudash and Capt. Al Meyer, his Electronic Warfare Officer (EWO, the back seat navigator in a Weasel aircraft) shot down by SAMs as the strike force crossed the Red River at the turn point (TP). Maj Dudash was one of our best Weasel pilots. In the short time we were at Takhli, Dudash had developed a good reputation as a Weasel pilot. Dudash, Meyer, and I went through jungle survival school in the same class when we arrived at Clark AFB, and then arrived at Takhli at the same time.

As our flight approached the Red River, I remember hearing the weasels calling out the SAM warnings. "We've got a SAM at 2 o'clock, 1 ringer, (pause) 3 ringer. He's getting ready to launch." I could hear my own Radar Homing and Warning (RHAW) gear giving the same warnings. Then the high pitch voice " there's one, there's two." I thought, "Christ, he's counting the SAMs being fired". I looked away from my Lead to about my 2 o'clock position and saw 2 huge orange balls exploding about 10 miles in front. Then the all important call, "there's three!" This time a huge orange and red blast appeared. I saw an F-105 being blasted to pieces and parts of airplane falling and burning all the way to the ground. Three orange balls marked the sky, as we, the last flight in the force of 4 flights of 4, approached the turn point at the Red River on our way to the target. As we passed the scene, the 3 orange balls were still there. Bits and pieces of F-105 were still burning on the ground in a huge ball of flame with smoke still rising from the fallen pieces trailing in the sky.

We pressed on and crossed the Red River doing about 500 Kts. We were really humming, trying desperately to stay up with the rest of the force, and remain in formation while listening to that awful screech of the beepers from the F-105 that had just been shot down, the warnings from our RHAW gear, Weasel warnings, and calls from other flights. It was deafening and eery! My first taste of real combat at its worst! We approached Thud Ridge and turned

*Pilots living quarters (Ponderosa) at Takhli Air Base, Thailand. 333 TFS pilots quartered at the Ponderosa get together on the patio during the Tet bombing halt in Feb '67. From front left-clockwise: Capt. Green; Capt. Alton Meyer (Dudash's back seat EWO) shot down with Dudash 26 Apr '67; Maj. John Dudash (Weasel pilot KIA 26 Apr '67); Capt. Bobby Martin (Weasel pilot and first to complete 100 missions as Weasel pilot at Takhli); Lt. Ed McCaffrey; Capt. Wally Brug; Lt. "Buddy" Jones; Lt. Gene "Hags" Haggerty.*

southeast. I remember being on the inside of the right turn as #2. 3 (Maj Ralph Kitchens) & 4 (Maj Jim Middelton) were on the outside of the turn, against the ridge. We rolled out and were paralleling the ridge on a heading toward the turn-point that would lead us to the Thermal Power Plant, 10 miles north of Hanoi. I was in the position to be looking into the ridge area. We were actually below the top of the ridge line and I thought, "So this is the infamous 'Thud Ridge'!

No sooner had we completed the turn, rolled out, when all of a sudden, I saw 2 Mig 17s pop over the ridge on about a 90 degree beam at our 10 o'clock position. I called them out to lead. Everything happened quickly! The Migs cut in front of us as though to attack the flight in front. They were falling in trail with the F-105s in front of us and lining up for a shot, right in front of us. I could not believe it! We were being engaged by some Mig 17s! I'd never seen a Mig for real, and at first I was fascinated to see my first Mig. It looked just like the pictures we had seen for aircraft identification training. I remember seeing a star on their fuselage.

When I first saw them, there were two, in formation, and in a slight left turn at about our 10 o'clock position, about a half mile. They were increasing their bank angle and appeared to not see our flight as they fell in trail with the flight in front of us. I was still amazed at seeing Migs. They really looked neat, I thought. Then the realization dawned on me that these Migs were here to shoot at us. They were not putting on an air show but were deadly serious, with weapons, intent on shooting us down.

Lead (Capt "Buddy" Jones) attempted to fire his 20MM gun but it jammed. He transmitted that his gun was jammed and directed me to get a shot off if I could. I slid out of wing formation, to the right for separation. I looked up into the windscreen and saw the Migs about a quarter mile in front of us . They were firing at the flight in front of us. I could see the 30MM red balls (Tracers) coming from their guns. It seemed like a slow rate of fire because only the red tracers were visible. I didn't have my site fixed for guns but rather for the bomb run which was about 40 mils (depressed), very low for any gun shot. I fired the gun anyway and ruddered the aircraft for a spray shot, but didn't hit anything. The Migs immediately broke right and disappeared to the south. I guess they finally realized they were being shot at and it scared the hell out of them. I rejoined in our loose formation as we continued on to the target.

We were approaching the end of Thud Ridge and the turn point which would lead us to the Power Plant further to the south. As we passed Phuc Yen airfield we started to pick up both 37AA and 57AA flak (white and grey puffs). I really didn't realize where it was coming from, but I remember it happened all of a sudden. Like instant cloud puffs! We went through it very quickly. I glanced at our airspeed about this time and of course we'd been in burner since we crossed the Red, indicating about 570 Kts.

We were really humming in minimum afterburner. I could see, as I glanced to our 1 or 2 o'clock, smoke billowing up from the bombs being dropped by the flights in front of us. We couldn't miss the target now since it was really being marked. The problem was, that we would not be able to see the target, precisely, to drop our bombs.

We arrived at the end of the ridge, the turn point. Lead initiated a right turn for our final run to the pop maneuver and the bomb run. He rolled out, dipped his left wing for me to cross over, in echelon formation for the roll in. I moved over quickly since I could feel we were really getting close to the target, and on my first pack 6 strike, I didn't want to screw it up. I was really excited and nervous. I didn't know what to expect during the bomb run with all the flak, Migs, SAM alerts, chatter and flak bursting all around us as we got closer to the target.

We started up in the pop maneuver for the bomb run. I was trying to stay in formation, in burner, and still trying to anticipate the roll-in which was about to occur. All of a sudden, Lead peeled off and rolled in for the bomb run. I followed and for the first time during this episode, I tried to see the target, the "Thermal Power Plant".

I knew I only had a few seconds to acquire the target, get the pipper on it with the right airspeed (450 Kts) and, 45 degree dive angle. Impossible task! Clouds of smoke and dust from 3 other flights which had dropped their bombs on the same place made acquiring the power plant almost impossible (4 A/C, X6/750lb bombs in each flight =24 bombs x 3 flights =72 bombs). This does not include the flak suppression flight's bombs that were exploding on the flak sites that were shooting at us located near the target.

All these explosions were occurring in a matter of only a couple of minutes which created one hell of a smoke, fire, and dust cloud. Lead's bombs had not hit yet when I acquired what I thought was the center of the Thermal Power Plant and pickled my bombs off. It was one hell of a mess to see through. I dropped my bombs, pulled hard to the right and off the target to join with lead. As I flew through a lot of smoke, dust, and debris, I wondered if I would pick up any foreign-object-damage (FOD) in the engine as a result. I quickly disregarded the thought because it seemed insignificant considering everything else going on. I really didn't have any choice.

I had to find lead, join on him, and get the hell out of there. I was in a weave, in a right turn off the target, then left, looking for Lead through the smoke, dust, and flak but did not see him. While in a right turn, I spotted an aircraft in my 11 o'clock position—it was a Mig 21, head-on to me and closing, but it had its gear down.

I thought that was odd, and as I looked down at the ground from my position, about 200 feet above the ground, doing about 500 Kts, I realized I was over Phuc Yen airfield. This guy was on final approach for landing! Flak was going off all over me, and although I couldn't see it, I knew they were shooting with small arms also. I took evasive action to avoid the Mig as a natural reflex. I was not armed to fire the gun and besides, not in any position to fire at the Mig anyway.

It was one hell of a site as the Mig past my 9 o'clock position. I wondered if he even saw me. My thoughts were again focused on finding Lead who should have been somewhere in front of me. I headed for Thud Ridge, our exit route.

Ralph Kitchens, our flight's number three man, called me and asked if I had Lead in sight? "Negative" was my reply. At that point, 3 said a Mig was on my tail and firing. I looked back over my right shoulder, and as I did, I saw red fire balls (tracers) passing me and further behind me was what I identified as a Mig 17. I could see the cannon near the right side of his fuselage lighting up as the red tracer rounds came out at a very slow rate. About every second, a fire ball would light up and stay lighted for a long time as they actually passed me, still lighted. Ralph rolled in on the Mig for a shot from my 7 o'clock and the Mig broke off immediately. At this point, I was really exhausted, scared, and sweating like crazy. I saw lead in front of me so I joined on his left wing, slid over to the right wing which put me against the side of Thud ridge. Ralph and his wingman, Jim Middelton, joined on the left wing. We were all joined and heading home as a flight!

Lead asked for a fuel check. I checked my gages and the adrenalin started to flow again. I really got scared because I only showed 3,000 pounds on the fuel gage. I thought, my God, I don't have enough fuel to make it to the tanker! I responded "Two has 3,000 Pounds"

There was silence, It was deafening because I knew what they were thinking. Lead asked me to repeat, and I did. 3 chimed in (Good ole Ralph) and said "check your circuit breaker." When we carried 6/750 lbs bombs, the internal bombay of the F-105 was equipped with a 350 gal tank (2,200 lbs of fuel) but it had to feed to the main tank which then fed the engine. A circuit breaker controlled the power to the pump that fed the fuel from the belly tank to the main tank. This circuit breaker was located right under the canopy rail on the left side, about left arm position, and under the canopy lock handle. It was very difficult to see when sitting in the cockpit. One had to lean forward, cock your head down, and look left under the canopy rail to see the circuit breaker panel where it is located. This breaker seemed to always pop with excessive G forces, and it was a common occurrence which had happened to me before in F-105 training at McConnell AFB.

Before I felt with my left hand and looked for the breaker, I thought, God, I hope that's it! Then I felt with my left hand to feel if one of the circuit breakers was sticking out and quickly looked to confirm what I felt or didn't feel. The breaker was out! Thank the Lord! I pushed it in and looked at my fuel gage to confirm that in fact it was the right breaker that would do the job because I could not really see which breaker I pushed in. The main tank fuel gage needle started to show an increase in fuel.

I cannot explain the absolute elation I felt when this occurred. I could have kissed Ralph. I was so panicked, I probably would not have thought of checking the circuit breaker.

After I was able to satisfy myself that I had enough fuel to get back to the tanker with the rest of the flight, I was able to regain my composure, somewhat. But what is strange is, I felt like nothing could touch me. I had survived my first pack 6 mission with everything they could throw at me—Migs attacked me, in and out, —shooting at me, SAMs, Flak all over the place, saw my friend shot down by a SAM, watched it explode, burn, flew over the flaming wreckage, and had an aircraft malfunction which I coped with. I felt untouchable! A very dangerous feeling! As scared as I was, I felt good. I didn't know it at the time, but the missions wouldn't get any easier.

"Jonsey", the flight lead, and I continued to check my fuel all the way back to the tanker, never really sure if I had a malfunction or if it was the popped circuit breaker that caused my problem. We refueled, and recovered to Takhli.

I had completed my first pack 6 mission! The debriefing was interesting too. They used all the information to update the target study folders which contained the flak and SAM sites, and any other information which may prove valuable for the next missions that were to follow. In addition, a bottle of whiskey was set in front of us with paper cups as "after mission whiskey". I needed it! I remember the paper cups melting from the whiskey as we sat there debriefing, not really drinking, but answering questions from the intelligence officer. Occasionally taking a sip of the whiskey while the cup practically melted. All the time I wondered about Dudash, and Al Meyer, his EWO (were they dead, captured, alive?) and the rest of the 67 missions I had left, and whether I would even finish 100 missions if all the rest are like this.

# Chapter Seven
# "Tomahawk 3," The Longest Mission
## 30 April, '67, Mission #34
## Hanoi Thermal Power Plant (10 Mi. North, Hanoi)

## Background

The aborted strike mission against Hanoi Thermal Power Plant in North Vietnam on 30 April, 1967 resulted in three F-105's, four pilots, including a Medal of Honor winner, being shot down. This mission has been written about in several different books or publications. "Thud Ridge", (The Longest Mission Chapter): "Going Downtown, the War Against Hanoi and Washington" both written by Col Broughton as well as "Modern Military Aircraft 'THUD', by Lou Drendel", and Air Force Magazine, to mention a few. In addition, excerpts have been taken from this episode and incorporated into other books about the Air War in Vietnam.

Major Leo Thorsness, Carbine 3, the Medal of Honor winner (Recommended at the time), had flown about 94 missions. Not many of us knew that Leo was recommended for the Medal of Honor for a mission he flew a few weeks earlier. As mentioned earlier, a completed tour in Southeast Asia was either flying 100 missions up north or one month deducted from a 12 month tour for each 20 in NVN. When 90 missions in the North were completed, however, there was an unofficial policy to schedule the last 10 missions in the lower route packs where the chances of being shot down were less. Leo elected to fly this mission even though he didn't need to fly a pack 6 mission again. He just wanted to finish and get out of there, and who could blame him.

That afternoon, this mission, led by the 355th TFW Vice Commander, Colonel Jack Broughton, was against the Hanoi Thermal Powerplant, located about seven miles north of Hanoi. The strike force was made up of twenty Thuds and four F-4 Phantoms, divided in our roles between bombers, Wild Weasels, and F-4 Mig CAP. When the force launched that afternoon, Leo Thorsness was the element Lead (#3) of the Weasel flight, "Carbine". The Weasel flight crews were as follows:

F-105F Carbine Lead:
    Major Ben Fuller, Pilot
    Captain Norm Frith, EWO

F-105F Carbine Two:
    Capt Joe Ritter, Pilot
    Capt John McGukin, EWO

F-105F Carbine Three:
    Major Leo Thorsness,
    Pilot (POW, this mission)
    Capt Harry Johnson,
    EWO (POW, this mission)

F-105D Carbine Four:
    Lt Bob Abbott
    (POW this mission)

*Major Ben Fuller*   *Capt. Norm Frith*   *Major Leo Thorsness*

Mission Force Commander, Col Broughton, designated Tomahawk (Flight of 4) as Rescue Flight for Carbine 3 & 4, as follows:

F-105D Tomahawk Lead      Major Ed Dobson
    Two      Capt Mike McCuistion (POW May 10)
    Three      Major Al Lenski
    Four      Capt Joe Abbott (POW this mission)

The original writing of this episode appeared in "Thud Ridge", "The Longest Mission" chapter. The information for this chapter was obtained from the audio tape which was recorded by the Lead Weasel, Carbine 1. The tape was given to me by Norm Frith, Carbine 1 EWO, later after the mission. Shortly before Col. Broughton left Takhli, he stopped by my quarters in the BOQ trailer and asked for a copy of the tape of Leo's shoot down. He wanted this particular mission to be a chapter in a book he planned to write about the war. It seemed like a great idea so I made a copy, with the help of Maj Ralph Kitchens, my trailer mate, and gave it to him.

"The Longest Mission" Chapter was mostly constructed from this tape recording. It factually relates the entire mission as it transpires from the audio tape recording, and of course, Col Broughton's personal involvement as the Force Commander (Waco Lead). Some transmissions however, were not recorded since Carbine flight (who recorded the mission) had exited the rescue area for refueling early in the rescue effort, and at times, was off the rescue frequency or out of reception range of transmissions from the rescap flight, Tomahawk, the pilots on the ground, and the Sandies.

In his Modern Military Aircraft book, "THUD", Lou Drendel, wrote the following paragraph regarding the Mig attack on myself (Tomahawk 3) & my wingman, Joe Abbott, #4 which occurred during the latter stage of the rescue effort.:

"....During this time, the North Vietnamese had launched Mig-21s. They were tracked by the airborne controllers, and spotted over Channel 97 by another flight, and it was probably one of these that shot down Tomahawk Four, adding yet another beeper to the din on guard frequency."

This incident occurred at the most critical part of the rescue mission since we were at the final stages of getting the rescue helicopters over the downed crews. What is missing from previous writings of this mission is the additional personal details from the on scene rescap flight, "Tomahawk". As I read about this mission in other publications, I felt I could fill in some details and gaps from my personal involvement during those final minutes, when in an instant, what looked like a successful rescue, turned into a complete disaster. As Tomahawk 3, I have attempted to recall the details of this episode from my memory, which is still vivid today, and the help of the audio tape of that mission.

We had remained over the downed pilots for about 40 minutes to provide air cover until the rescue Sandies (A-1's) and rescue helicopters arrived. Throughout those last few agonizing minutes of the rescue effort, Tomahawk 1 & 2, (Maj Dobson and Capt McCuistion) provided low cover while myself and Joe Abbott (Tomahawk 3 & 4), provided radio relay above them. Our location was over the Red River at 15 thousand feet in a racetrack pattern, 30 miles west of Hanoi, in the vicinity of Phu Tho. That is, until Joe and I were attacked by Mig 21's and Joe (Tomahawk 4) became the third F-105 to be shot down, and finally the rescue effort terminated without success.

## "How I Remember 'The Longest Mission' as Tomahawk 3"

30 April, 1967, "The Longest Mission", my 34th, and 2nd mission to pack 6. This was the same target as my first pack 6 mission, the Hanoi Thermal Power Plant, only 3 days earlier. It was a JCS fragged target. I remember thinking, "they really want this target destroyed" or probably what is more accurate, "they did not know how bad we destroyed it three days ago, or, they really are not paying attention to the bomb damage assessment on the target."

My thoughts were, "we had completely destroyed the power plant already. What else did Washington or 7th Hdq want? Don't they know the risk in going back there again? Don't they know the defenses around that place? All we'll do is drop more bombs on a target we've already destroyed and lose some more pilots and F-105's doing it."

I had a hard time following the higher headquarters logic to go back to the same targets so soon after they had already been put out of commission. This was my first reservation about how this war was being fought. About who was running the show and who made the decisions on targets to be hit, etc. I found myself questioning these decisions as my tour went on, and frankly, didn't like what was happening. I always felt I had a firm grasp of why we were there and did not have a problem with those reasons. But I was having second thoughts about the way the U.S. chose to fight this war as a military arm of the U.S. which should be to try to win as quickly as possible. At least that's what we had been taught at Air Command and Staff College (ACSC), the U.S. Air Forces professional military school for future Air Force leaders. I did not understand the logic of our target selection, and the multitude of restrictions put on the air war we were being asked to fight up north. It seemed like a "negative war". It appeared our leaders were tying our hands behind our backs and asking us to fight an enemy who had many vulnerable areas but few of those areas or targets were allowed to be touched—by our own making.

I remember the night before this mission after I found out I was scheduled as Tomahawk 3. I kept thinking about the last time I went to the Thermal Power Plant. It was a morning mission and we had a lot of flak over the target, Migs and SAMs and worst of all we'd lost a weasel aircraft, and two pilots, friends of mine. This however, was an afternoon mission. I didn't have to get up early, so that evening I decided to go to Wing Operations where the flight planning for our missions took place. I wanted to look at the target maps, intelligence reports, and just get some target study time. I was nervous as hell!

I happen to see Col Jack Broughton in the planning room at Wing Hdqs. He was to be the Force Commander for the mission, and he was already there doing some planning and thinking about this mission himself. I was impressed! We discussed the mission and the routes in and out etc. He wanted to ingress a different way this time instead of the same way we had been going in on all the other missions. He felt we had to alter our ingress and not be predictable. It sounded like a good idea to me. Since I was new to pack 6 missions, I was trying to learn as much as I could from the guys with experience.

I assisted in getting information for him and the usual planning things to help the guy who is making the decisions. His plan was to ingress directly to the Power Plant via Phu-Tho, located on the Red River (a large looping bend in the river which was an excellent check point), only miles from Hanoi and the power plant. He planned to hit the target going north and egress out the ridge to the northwest. This was exactly the opposite from our routine ingress routes of the past. Not a bad idea! At least it would keep the bastards honest!

The next day, I awaited the afternoon mission hanging around Wing Ops looking at the mission maps which, incidentally, were always planned by a different flight the night before. We waited for the morning force to return from pack 6 to see what the results were and how our guys made out. It was lunch time!

*Takhli Officers Club. Served as primary eating, bar, gathering place for pilots. Meals were served any hour of the day, 24 hrs/day. Home away from home for pilots.*

CS **RAINBOW** | SE 1344 | TAXI 1382 | TO 1419 | TOT 1520 | SE 70

| | | | | | |
|---|---|---|---|---|---|
| 1 ME | 173 | A-1 | TOR 6700 | NWLO 8/3 | TOS 173 |
| 2 GENE | 109 | B-2 | LS 105 /2M | MAX REF 148/158 | |
| SP FRANK | 478 | A-11 | SAR 14 | P 364.2S 282.8 | |
| 4 | 159 | | CROWN/SANDY/JOLLY GREEN | | |
| SP | 522 | B-23 | MIG SQUID | | |
| | | | SAM BELT BUCKLE | | |

A CS BA71 ARCT 1450 190/7.5 — 6x750 I/01 1/3 T.D.-24
AAR PCN 11 S 336.8 278.0 — 93 29.71/69

TGT 8530 CODE REACTOR — Bree 3M
COORD 2018/10435 — 331.2 ...
ELEV WINDS P — 2 & ... 4 sec.
ALT STG S

TGT 917A CODE GALLAHAD
COORD 2113/10255 — BORD VIOL WEEKEND
ELEV WINDS P — EXEC TEACOP BUMBLE BEE / SKI BOOT
ALT STG S — CANX CORKSCREW / YOUNGSTOWN PASSBOOK
TGT RPI RED CODE KEEGLER — TOT / CHG CANADIANS / BASE TIME
COORD — RECALL TOUCH BACK
ELEV WINDS 28/18 P — WX FLIPPER
ALT STG 29.54 S — SUCESS BARKEEP
UNSUCC PATROL
DIVERT FRANKINSTEIN

DO Form 1, Jan 66

*Mission line-up card. A flight of two aircraft. Note that only first names or nicknames were used on these cards since they were carried on our knee pad in the cockpits. Last names were not to be used in case the North Vietnamese recovered these cards from the wreckage of a shoot down. This card list "Me" and "Gene" (Gene "Hags" Haggerty) as my wingman. The "spare" for this mission is also listed as Frank and a spare aircraft is also listed. Everything is coded and the codes were changed each mission.*

Lunch time was not a pleasant time for me. I couldn't eat anything. I wasn't hungry, but I always tried to force myself to eat something. The thought that this may be my last chance to eat a meal always nagged at me. I new I should eat to keep my strength up. Most of the strike force pilots congregated at the O'Club about the same time for lunch. You usually could tell who was on the upcoming mission. The guys who flew the morning mission were always living it up, but the guys getting ready for the afternoon mission were dead serious only making an effort to be jolly and laughing it up. I could tell the difference! I could feel the tension at the tables and the occasional blank stares. Thoughts of family, friends, some self confessing, half joking, that if they don't come back, "have a party on the money I leave in my wallet", etc. Everyone seemed to have their own way to handle or deal with the "next pack 6 mission" and the reality of the odds of not coming back facing them.

I think I probably dealt with this in a quiet way. I didn't like to talk about it much, and wanted to maintain a positive, strong attitude about it, but it was difficult for me. I tried to think that "I'm the best, I can make it if I do my homework, study the target area maps and defenses, flak, and SAM maps, obey the lessons learned, and don't take unnecessary chances, accept only good airplanes whose systems are working properly and make good pre-flights before you climb into the cockpit for the mission". Once in the hostile area, "keep it fast, keep it moving and keep your head on a swivel with your eyes open and always keep checking six".

Briefing time was approaching, and the guys at the club started to trickle out, headed for Wing Ops and the briefing. Most of the pilots stuck together as flights. Each Squadron had a Pick-up-Truck assigned, so we normally used the truck to travel together as a flight . When we arrived at Ops, you could feel the tension build. Things started to really get serious. Pilots were preparing and studying maps, making last minute notes on the mission cards, folding their maps so they fit comfortably for easy access in the cockpit.

As an aside, maps and mission cards were prepared for 3 different missions the night before. The Primary, 1st, and 2nd alternate. As mentioned earlier, the pilots flying the mission usually did not prepare the maps and cards for the mission. A different flight was tasked to flight plan for a full week, each night before the next days mission. Their duties were to flight plan and prepare the target maps and cards after the Frag Order arrived from higher headquarters listing the next days targets. So planning took place around 7 o'clock in the evening until you finished, which was usually around 10 o'clock. All the maps, charts, and cards were prepared for each member of the flight and put into the respective flight bins for the next days mission.

The Wing had also established a Squadron scheduling procedure which worked pretty well. Each Squadron had 4 flights. One flight assigned to primary flying, one to secondary flying, one to flight planning, and one was off (R&R). The R&R flight was "forced". That is, when that flight was scheduled for R&R, those pilots were not allowed to fly. The policy was to take a week's break. No if and no "buts" about it. Flight planning week usually was followed by the flying week which peaked you up, then a back-up flying week which let you down slowly, then R &R. It worked very well.

I reviewed the mission board to get an overview of who was leading the force. This was important to know, from my perspective, and in addition, to know who were the flight leaders and any other really good friends who might be on the mission.

Col Broughton was still assigned to Lead the force of 5 flights of 4 F-105's, so I assumed the ingress route was as he had planned it the night before. Maj Ed Dobson was leading our flight with Mike McCuistion; as Tomahawk 2 . I was 3 with Joe Abbott as my wingman. At the time, I really didn't know Joe that well. He was assigned as one of the Safety Officers in Wing Hdq. and was attached to our Squadron (333 TFS) for flying. As I recall, Joe didn't have a lot of experience but had a good reputation. Mike was new with fewer missions than I. Dobson was an old head, experienced, and with a reputation as one of the best. He was known to take chances and press at times, but that is not necessarily bad. Once, he brought back some jungle under the belly of his F-105 and was admonished by the Commander for pressing a strafing run. As a result he was taken off Flight Lead status to cool his heels. The "Dober" was good!

Briefing time arrived, and we all took our maps and cards into the huge Wing briefing room and waited to hear the weather briefing and await the "execution words" for the afternoon mission. I always hated waiting for "Words". It kept you on a string, so to speak. That is, the pack 6 mission was always the primary target and depending on the weather, as decided by 7th Hdq, we may or may not "be executed on the primary target". If the Weather was marginal for visibility or clouds in the Hanoi area, we went to one of the alternate targets. This mission wasn't any different. We waited, and waited! All 24 of us plus the briefers and others who wanted to listen assembled in the briefing room, seated by flights and by position in the flight (1,2,3,4). A full house!

We received our weather and intelligence briefings (by the Intelligence officer and weatherman) on the ingress and target area defenses, active SAM sites, flak sites, best escape and evasion safe routes, and Mig threat. We were shown the latest Recce Photos of the target area and the precise area we were to hit at the Thermal Power Plant. Everything was covered by everybody. Now, all we wanted to know was, what target will we be executed on.

Usually the way it happened was one of the intelligence officers would get the "Words" from 7th Air Force by phone in another room, and then enter the rear entrance door to the briefing room and flash a signal to the Force Commander who was at the front of the briefing room. The signal was in the form of holding up 1, 2 or 3 fingers. Number one meant PRIMARY-DOWNTOWN, and two, first alternate, etc. This period of waiting for execution orders was in my opinion, the most difficult.

Usually, the room was silent! It stayed that way for long periods of time, each pilot having his own personal thoughts and reflections. You could hear a pin drop—literally! Then you heard the door in the back of the briefing room open, and you knew what was coming. If you had guts, you looked back to see for yourself, otherwise stare forward for the news from the Force Commander who would say something like, "O.K. guys, PRIMARY", or Secondary etc. Once the ice was broken and we knew where we were going, you felt better because you could start really psyching yourself up for pack 6 or actually feeling more relaxed about going to a lower route pack instead.

When PRIMARY was announced on this mission, you could hear the shuffling of feet, and murmur crack the silence. In this case, now that we knew we were going "Primary", the thought hit me that the odds were that some of the guys in this room weren't coming back, and everyone in the room knew it. It was a tense time! In my view, it was the most stressful time during the whole process of briefing and getting ready for a mission.

Col Broughton got up and proceeded to brief us on any last minute thoughts he had. He had already briefed the mission in detail but he had a few words about the new route, to remind us of the new ingress routing and why. Then reiterated the rescue procedures in case someone got shot down. The phrase, "ANY QUESTIONS?" finished the briefing and no one had any! We knew what we had to do, it was routine for pack 6, and not anything special as far as we knew. Unfortunately, we didn't know what was in store for us on this mission nor how bad this mission would turn out.

We adjourned, and each flight in the Wing went separate ways to their Squadron briefing rooms to brief their own flights on individual flight procedures. This took about another 20 minutes after you got back to your Squadron building. Time was still available after this briefing before going to the Personal Equipment room which was the last contact with anyone.

Here we got our parachute, G suit, and other paraphernalia for the mission. Rings came off, wallets and personal belongings were stored. Only your military I.D. card, some North Vietnamese money, (supposedly to buy your way out if you got shot down and captured, that is, if you could con some North Vietnamese to get you out with money) was carried.

A routine was followed by most guys. I always did my flight dressing preparation in the same fashion, same sequence, paying attention to habit. Same thing all the time! Wedding ring off, wallet out and stored, all U.S. change and other coins and personal items out of pockets and put on the open shelf of the locker space each of us had. All perfectly aligned on the shelf. I wanted it that way in case I didn't come back. G suit on, 38 pistol, ammo with tracers, survival vest checked for all the survival gear. The battery operated emergency radio (which was personal) was removed from the survival vest we wore and given to the Personal Equipment (PE) airman to check for operation. He'd run a check on the radio for a good beeper and battery life, then give it back or replace the battery. When all personal survival items were in order and in the right pockets of the G suit and vest, I was ready to go except for checking the helmet and oxygen mask, and parachute. This last check was routine with the P. E. specialist. Now, I was ready to walk out the door to the airplane.

The early morning missions were something to behold. It was dark, crickets, frogs (a lot of them) and all the night sounds were there. We had to cross a little trench full of water which separated the flight line ramp with a walkway from the Wing Hdq and Squadron building areas. The sound of frogs croaking was enormous, and I'll never forget that sound. For me, it is synonymous with flying pack 6 missions, even today! This particular mission was in the afternoon but I could still hear the frogs croaking as I crossed the trench-way onto the ramp, to my aircraft. Loaders were scooting around in their little bomb loader machines with bombs and ammo, and the flight line was alive with traffic and maintenance personnel. The sound of ground power units was deafening.

I proceeded to my F-105 loaded down with all my gear, carrying my helmet, maps and mission cards. I also carried a flight bag of letdown charts and checklists just in case I needed it for any diversions in flight. I guess it served more as a security blanket than anything else.

The routine was always the same. Arrive at the aircraft, meet the crew chief and look at the Form 781 (aircraft maintenance status form for each aircraft) for discrepancies, ask whatever questions you had about the airplane and strike up a friendly conversation. I always tried to take my mind off the mission as much as possible during this time. The crew chiefs were great! Most of the time they knew where we were going. Even if they knew, they would always ask where we were going. I don't know of a crew chief that wasn't dedicated, "absolutely", to making sure we had a good airplane to fly into combat.

TFS Operations Building across from flight line at Takhli. Each Sqd (2 others 354 TFS, & 357 TFS) had same type buildings. Thai grounds-keeper maintaing the garden appearance in lower left of photo.

I often wished I could trade places with them as I started to climb up the ladder, into the cockpit. This mission was no different. I thought, "How lucky you are and you probably don't even know what I'm thinking!" I had a few tell me

Flight Line at Takhli viewed from Squadron Operations building. Visible trenches, usually filled with water, housed many frogs, snakes and crickets that made for an awesome sound during early morning missions. Maintenance shacks, left center of photo housed the maintenance personnel for quick access to aircraft. Jet blast fences are visible at right center of photo which blocks view of some F-105s. A "Weapons Loader" vehicle is visible at far right in back of Jet Blast fence.

how lucky they felt that they did not have to fly these missions we were going on. They always wished us luck as they finished helping us strap into the cockpit and then retreated down the ladder and took it away. I've had a few who had tears welling up in their eyes while strapping me in and talking about anything, just to keep talking. I could see the fear and whatever feelings they had, pouring out. Sometimes, it made me feel stronger. I don't know why. I thought, "They don't know the half of it. If they only knew how I felt, only knew the half of it!" I was scared as hell and they didn't even know it! We were "fighter pilots", guys who were supposedly God Almighty", I guess. I had real news for them, but then you don't spill your guts to the crew chief.

Routinely, I preflighted the aircraft, climbed in, got strapped in, and the crewchief left with a "good luck" and a salute. Now I was alone, and ready to start at the designated time. After starting the engine, doing all the after start checks and aligning the gun/bomb sight, I was ready for check in with Tomahawk flight and the rest of the strike force. I remember an emergency beeper going off on guard frequency so I turned the guard receiver off to hear the "check-in" call. A beeper going off on guard happened occasionally when the PE guys were checking out the survival radios in the nearby squadron areas, so I didn't pay much attention to it. We finally all got checked in, taxied out, took off and were on our way to pack 6 and the Hanoi Power Plant.

As usual, the KC-135 refueling tankers had taken off earlier and so had the RB-66s, the Weasels, and we, the four flights of four bomb flights were now on our way with the Strike Force intact. Rendezvous with the tankers was normal as we took on fuel and proceeded down the refueling track, cycling on and off the tanker to keep a full load of fuel in everyone. We finally reached the drop-off point with each aircraft sucking the last bit of gas it could take. Each flight dropped off the tanker, and as we departed the tankers, we got our usual farewell from the tanker folks- "Good hunting and Good luck, see you on the way out!"

"God, I envied them", as they did a 180 degree turn and headed back for their holding points in Thailand until we came back out for post strike refueling.

"Clean 'em up, and green 'em up" calls were made (clean up the refueling switches and arm the weapon switches, check for "green arm lights) as we descended to clear the tankers, headed north for the turn point (Phu Tho) that would then lead us to the "Hanoi Power Plant" from the south.

This is where the mission gets heated up with all the radio calls, being made as we ingressed to the target. The F-4s, our Mig Cap, started to join-up with us as we dropped off the tankers. They were desperately trying to get into a Mig-cover position by positioning themselves with two F-4's in front of our strike force and two in back, both high. The weasels (Carbine flight), about 30 miles in front of us, were already picking up SAM signals as we pressed toward channel 97 TACAN station for our last doppler (navigation equipment) fix. Fixing the doppler updated the navigation system to give us the last accurate position from which the navigation system would use to now "deadreckon" (extrapolate) range and bearing to a selected point, across the Black River, toward the Red River, Phu Tho check point, and then the Power Plant target.

All the flights were jockeying, trying to get into the proper formation position which was about a mile in trail of each other, stacked low, from the strike force leader to the last flight in the string. We (Tomahawk) were the last flight in that string of 4 flights. I was on the right side of the flight as element lead with #4 (Joe Abbott) hanging on to my right wing in loose route formation. We were headed NNE, so I was looking west, away from the high threat area of Hanoi and the target area.

The Weasels were now calling SAM threats and my Radar Homing And Warning equipment (RHAW) was giving me fits. I was getting Mig signals, SAM warnings, the Yellow SAM warning light (SAM lock on) and a few SAM launch lights (Red), but nothing happened. I began not to trust the RHAW signals, the associated warning lights and aural warnings. I turned it off and decided that listening to the Weasels and the flight leads was better information. Besides, as an element Lead in the last flight, I hardly felt like my input would make any difference.

We were progressing down the track, and I remember seeing the Black River going by underneath and thinking how wide and muddy it looked and that it made a good check point for time distance/dead reckoning on future missions when the doppler navigation system wasn't functioning. Shortly after we crossed the Black River, I saw two aircraft about 10 o'clock, 6 to 8 miles, going the other way, (180 degrees from our direction) as though they were exiting the area. I thought that was funny, "only two aircraft." We always went to pack 6 in a force and at least a flight of four to pack five which in this case was possible from our position. I called "bogies at 10 o'clock".

On the audio tape of this mission, it is very garbled and hard to identify who made the call but I believe that to be the call-out I made at that time. Very quickly thereafter, Col Broughton (the force leader) directed a channel change to strike frequency. I waited for my leader to tell us to change frequency, but he never did. Everyone switched frequencies on the Force Lead's call but me.

As I listen to the tape, all the flights checked in but me, and after a short time, Dobson came back to the frequency to pick me up. I switched frequency and checked in. In the mean time, I worried about the bogies I called out but no one acknowledged the call. I started to think, "Maybe I don't understand how this force operation is supposed to work."

I still believe that those two aircraft were Migs, and that they were the ones who shot down Carbine 3 & 4 shortly thereafter. We just kept humming on. Radio calls, SAM warnings from the Weasels, F-4 Mig-Cap talking about dropping their tanks and good ole Mig warnings from the Navy off shore with coordinates which didn't make sense anyway, in addition to a stray beeper on guard frequency going off. The chatter on the radio frequency increased. The noise level in the headset was unbearable. We were getting close to the RED, pack 6, and Hanoi.

After I made the call about the Bogies at 10 o'clock, the tape reflects that Carbine 1 did pick up on the call and asked, "who said what" on their internal Communications. But no one else paid attention as we approached Phu Tho, the Red River Initial Point (IP) for our final run in to the target with a lot of SAM and FAN SONG (Radar Control Site) warnings.

Then, the most important transmission from Joe Ritter, Carbine 2 is audible and missed by all. He apparently sees Carbine 4 (Bob Abbott) out of his peripheral vision being shot down and sees the flames. He calls it out to Carbine 1 on strike frequency, but again no one pays attention. Carbine 1 probably didn't hear this call because of all the SAM activity and internal communication in his cockpit which can be heard on the tape. Only by listening closely, a couple of times to the tape can the sequence of calls and internal communication be understandable. Apparently no one else saw what had happened either. It was the ultimate clue that Migs were at Carbine's six o'clock and moving forward trying to pick them off one by one. The transmission from Carbine 2 was missed!

Carbine flight presses on but not for long. The SAM warnings were increasing in intensity and numbers. All being called to the strike force by Carbine Lead. Both, he (Ben Fuller) and his "Bear" (the back seat EWO, Norm Frith) were busy as hell. Internal communication, Guard reception, and Strike force Communication are all coming in at once and when that happens it's hard to weed out the wheat from the chaff. Things are happening fast, a lot of chatter is going on. That's how it normally was in pack 6 with all the defenses coming up at once and 24 fighters on one frequency. Pick out the important calls and ignore the rest. Stay alert, and listen intently for significant calls. I for one was listening to the Weasels alerting us of the threats and for any calls from Tomahawk lead.

Carbine 1 warned the Force of some threats with, "Fan Song looking at us at 12 o'clock". Then the deafening call " 1 1/2 rings. "Carbines, he's looking at us!".

About 5 seconds after this call, this transmission came in loud and clear, **"This is Carbine 3, I've flamed out , Carbine 3, I've flamed out, MAYDAY, MAYDAY, MAYDAY"**. There was no mistake about missing this call or seeing the aircraft being shot out of the sky.

Despite the confusion at this point, Carbine 1 displayed real professionalism under the most difficult circumstances. It almost sounds routine. The tape went into chip monk talk immediately, as Carbine 1 lays the Gs on, causing the audio tape-recorder in the cockpit to drag from the excessive G force.

Carbine 1 advised Leo (Carbine 3) to **"Get out" "Get out"**! He was burning bad and going down in flames. Leo probably didn't need Carbine 1 to tell him to get out. Immediately, two chutes came into view and Carbine 1 Bear (Norm Frith) says, in a hurried and excited voice, "I got two chutes, I got two chutes, look at the chutes, look at the chutes"!

Leo Thorsness and his EWO, Harry Johnson (Carbine 3) were on their way to either being rescued, captured, or being killed. The air filled with excitement. Waco Lead (Col Broughton), the Strike Force Commander, made an immediate decision to cancel the mission and devote the force to getting the downed guys out.

Some conversation took place between Carbine and Waco and then the Emergency Beepers started screeching. The sound was unbearable! Flights were talking, two beepers were going off, and all hell was breaking loose. The only way to communicate was to turn off the Guard frequency.

At this point, Carbine Lead called his flight to Channel 14, rescue frequency.

The Airman
Magazine 1987.

Ben was trying to get the correct coordinates of the downed crews to pass to Crown, the rescue coordinator. The beepers continued. You could hear Leo and Harry, who were now on the ground, come up on the survival radio on Guard frequency. They are told to get up the hill by Carbine 1, that they have them in sight and see both chutes. The beepers keep going! and going! I thought, "God, if they'd only stop!" Carbine advises Leo to "Get up the hill some," and that "We're taking ground fire from the bottom of the hill."

Carbine 1 tried to call Crown (the rescue coordinator) and Waco flight (the Force leader) but couldn't seem to raise anyone. Ben and Norm were worried and sounded panicky. Ben (Carbine 1) on internal communication says, "Where is everyone"? Shortly after Carbine 1 tells Waco Lead that they think they have a beeper activated in their flight, which is really Carbine 4 (Bob Abbott) who has already been shot down and don't know it yet, Carbine flight is ordered out of the area by Waco Lead (Col Broughton). Things are confusing as hell at this point because no one knows that Carbine 4 has also been shot down and that his beeper is still sounding off.

A short time later, as Carbine is leaving the area for refueling, Carbine 1 attempted to get his number 4 to check in and when 4 doesn't respond, he becomes concerned about his whereabouts.

When Crown (Rescue coordinator) asks Waco lead to designate a high flight for communication relay and Rescap purposes, Col Broughton designates Tomahawk as the rescue flight to stay in the area while the rest of the force exits the area for refueling and relief if needed later.

At this point, Dobson and McCuistion (Tomahawk 1&2) assumed low cover and, for all practical purposes, were functioning as an independent element of two, over the downed crews. Myself and Joe Abbott (Tomahawk 3 & 4) climbed above them to 15 thousand feet to provide radio relay as a separate element.

The coordinates of downed Carbine 3 & 4 were given to the rescue coordinator (Crown) by Carbine 1 as 2118N, 10500E. When Crown asked how long the rescue flight could stay in the area, Dobson, Tomahawk Lead, estimated we could stay in the area about 45 minutes (A reasonable estimate).

Waco Lead tells Carbine to ask the Tankers to move further north and Carbine acknowledges.

Carbine, now on the way to the tanker, keeps asking Carbine 4 to check in, but has no luck.

Finally Carbine 2, Joe Ritter, asks 1 to go to channel 13 for a "conference". Joe Ritter tells Ben Fuller that he thought 4 got shot down just before Leo did. Joe says, "I looked behind me and saw two balls of flame, looked like a split airplane falling in pieces or two drop tanks on fire just before Leo getting hit . I called to you a couple seconds before Leo getting hit but I didn't know if you heard me or not." A short dead silence is followed by Ben's and Norm's internal conversation which is heard on their audio cockpit tape.

The words of Carbine 1, Ben Fuller, on internal Communication is, "Oh F_ _ _ !", and Norm Frith returns with, "Jesus Christ!" That kind of said it all! The total frustration and confusion that existed. But bless their souls, they come right back into the confused mess and called Crown to relay this information—immediately.

As Carbine 1 proceeded to the tanker, relaying as much information as they had, the internal communication between Ben and Norm is as expected. "What happened to us? Who shot Leo down? Where is 4, etc?"

This is where Carbine's aircraft (radio & tape recorder), because of distance, goes out of contact with what is going on over the rescue area on the Red River, just west of Phu Tho. They were trying to rendezvous with a tanker about 100 miles to the south but not having very good luck from the conversation on the tape. By the time Carbine refueled and returned to the rescue area, a lot went on.

I had set up a racetrack pattern at 15 thousand feet over the rescue area, just above Tomahawk 1 & 2. I tried to establish a 2 min leg, inbound to Phu Tho on sort of a , SE, NW heading along the Red River. I kept looking back over my shoulder, as far back as I could, to check our 6 o'clock position and #4, Joe Abbott. Each time it seemed as though Joe was lagging back. This concerned me, and I remember reminding him to "move it up". I worried about us holding at this medium altitude (15,000 ft) for this length of time, only 30 miles from Hanoi and 25 miles from Phuc Yen Airfield where they had Mig 21s and 17s. In addition, Yen Bai, one of Vietnam's active SAM sites was only about 15 miles away. I could see Phuc Yen airfield, the city of Hanoi, and Gia Lam Airfield. I felt like I was in their holding pattern for an instrument approach.

After about 20 minutes of rescaping, we got a call from Crown saying they have a report of "sighted" Migs over Channel 97 which was our TACAN station just south of the North Vietnam border in Laos. Crown said the Migs were approaching the area and about 40 miles out.

I heard the call but did not put a lot of trust in the sighting because CH 97 was south of us and only about 10 miles south of the North Vietnam border, in Laos. It didn't make sense with all the U.S. aircraft flying around that area during the rescue effort that they could determine who was flying where. It seemed like a bad report.

What I believe was detected, was Carbine flight (F-105's) coming back in the area to relieve us. (I still believe the report was not accurate). Besides, I felt we were staying here till we got Leo and his "Bear" (Harry) out anyway. This was good info and at least, I thought, someone was paying attention to our situation. I tucked the information away and tried to keep my eyes open, head on a swivel, keep an eye on my wingman, and constantly check our 6 o'clock area, just in case I was wrong and the report was right.

After about 30 minutes of rescaping, "Carbine called to say he was inbound, 42 miles out trailing the Sandies in. I thought, "Good, some relief is on the way because we're getting low on fuel, approaching our minimum fuel requirement of 4,000 lbs (Bingo fuel) to join with a tanker for refueling further south.

An interesting call from Oakland Flight to Crown revealed that the Migs reported earlier were not Migs. Crown acknowledged. I heard it, and thought, "I'm right, they were not Migs after all."

As Carbine 1 & 2 started to enter the rescue area near the Red river, Ben and Norm (Carbine 1) get into it as a 3 ringer and SAM launch is detected. The exchange between both is heated but professional. It sounded like they were getting frustrated and tired.

We'd (Tomahawk flight) been in the rescue area for at least 30 minutes by then. The frequencies were filled with the sound of screeching beepers when the Sandies finally arrived in the area. Tomahawk 1 & 2 just below me were trying to get the Sandies to make visual contact with the downed pilots so the Helicopters could be called in for rescue, but the Sandies couldn't visually locate the downed pilots or the chutes. This went on for at least 10 minutes and became very frustrating. The beepers were continuous and everybody was talking on the radio, both Guard and the main frequency. You could hardly hear yourself think.

Dobson, Tomahawk 1, was really getting frustrated by now since he could not seem to get the Sandies to see the downed pilots even as they flew right over them. We'd been in the rescap mode now for about 40 minutes.

A this point, fuel remaining was becoming a problem for all of us. My wingman, Joe Abbott, Tomahawk 4, called me to declare "Bingo fuel." I looked at my fuel gage, and I had 4 thousand pounds of fuel also.

I knew this was barely enough to get back to the tanker from the target area. Some quick calculations of fuel burn and estimated time to the tanker seemed to me that we should still have enough fuel to get to the tanker with some reserve. So I thought I would make one more round (What a mistake!) and if nothing happened, we'd have to leave or run out of fuel. Besides, I could always punch the tanks off if we really got in a bind, but that wouldn't allow us to be used for rescap again if this thing lasts that long. What I didn't count on, was having to use the afterburner during a Mig engagement which was about to occur in the next few minutes.

We were heading away from Phu Tho, on a westerly heading. Tomahawk 1 (Dobson) was still trying desperately to vector the Sandies into a position so they could locate Carbine 3 & 4 on the ground, but the "Dober" was not having much luck. Carbine 1&2 were almost back into the area, trying to get set up to relieve us in the rescap effort. The way things were unfolding now, it seemed that in a few minutes, we'd be relieved by Carbine flight and on our way to the tankers. The Sandies would have the downed pilots in sight, and the Helicopters would have them out in no time flat. (Wrong!)

I turned left for a 180 degree turn toward the east, and during the turn, I could see Phu Tho, the big bend in the Red river, and Hanoi further to the east. It was hazy and getting late in the afternoon with some scattered puffy clouds below us starting to build up. The beepers and chatter continued at an ear deafening level.

I had only acknowledged Joe's minimum fuel call but did not tell him what I planned to do. I know he probably wondered what my plan was. I'd planned this to be our last racetrack pattern turn. The next turn would be for home. We flew for another 2 minutes and I started another left turn toward the southwest.

Carbine 1 then made this transmission. "Sandy, Carbine 3 is calling you on guard, If you could answer him, he'd appreciate it." At this point, **all hell broke loose!** This is what is heard immediately after that transmission and in a high pitched, excited voice.

**"Break Right, —Tomahawk!  Migs, behind you!"** (This was my wingman, Joe Abbott, Tomahawk 4 trying to alert me of the Migs)

Just as I started that left turn to the southwest, within a couple of split seconds before that transmission, I heard this loud explosion, **"BANG!"** Simultaneously, my F-105 was on its back and I was staring down at the ground, upside down. It was so quick! Everything happened so quick. I mean, within fractions of a second, The BANG!, and immediately the aircraft rolled inverted! My immediate thought was that Joe ran into me. He'd been lagging and I kept trying to bring him forward throughout the flight. My reaction was to roll back to level flight.

The gear warning horn was blowing, and I had some yellow caution and Red Emergency lights on, but I didn't have time to find out what they were. Within a second or two of being hit, I heard the call, "Break Right, —Tomahawk! Migs, behind you!". They weren't behind me anymore because as I looked up, and to my right, I saw a Mig 21, silver, with red stars. I was canopy to canopy with him and I could see the Mig pilot in the cockpit. the Mig 21 was in a left bank, sliding high to my 2 o'clock position. I looked the other way, left and high. There was another Mig 21 sliding high at about 10 o'clock. They had us in a perfect sandwich! I saw Joe back about my 8 o'clock and a little low. At this point, I knew we'd had it!

Tomahawk 1 (Dobson) responded with, "Which Tomahawk has Migs?" This only took about 5 seconds from the time I was hit and Joe made his "break right" call. I immediately transmitted that I was hit, that there were Migs in the area and I was heading South. I asked Joe if he had me and the Migs in sight. He replied that he had me in sight and that he was O.K.

My assessment of the situation was that I had to get away, quick. Warning lights were on, the gear horn was blowing, and I didn't know how bad I'd been hit. I didn't have time to assess the damage and as long as I was flying, I really didn't care. I knew that as low as I was on fuel, my only option was to disengage, not fight. I was outnumbered, at a disadvantage, with an unassessed damaged aircraft, low on fuel, and in their back yard.

I punched the mike button and blurted again that I was hit, moving it around and again, that there were Migs in the area and I was heading south. I was scared as hell! I wanted someone to know I'd been hit and that we were engaged by Migs. If I had to eject, I wanted the rescue guys to know where I was and what was happening.

Many things went through my mind quickly, like, how to handle this situation. I remember that the Migs had Infra-Red, heat seeking, (IR, ATOL) missiles, and that's what they probably shot at me. It must have exploded on a proximity fuse, and if I could get into the clouds below and stay in them long enough, the Mig won't be able to lock on to me nor will an IR missile guide very well in the clouds where the heat source is diffused. I also didn't believe the guy would be able to pick me up on radar again, lock on, and have time to launch with enough overtake for a <u>radar</u> missile to guide either. It was a survival situation! Me against those two damn Mig 21s. I still thought I could get away, if I could only get into the clouds below.

I dove down and pulled hard to the right, into the Mig on my right side who was above and to the right about 3 o'clock. I lit the burner to accelerate and to get into the clouds as quick as I could. I wanted to get underneath the Mig so he could not see me. As I maneuvered to the clouds below, I asked Joe if he still had me. He replied that he did and said "keep going." I was indicating about 550 Kts and accelerating quickly and then remembered that I still had the 450 gal fuel tanks on. I also remembered the airspeed restriction on jettisoning the tanks to be 350 Kts in level flight, unloaded (no Gs) or the tanks might take the horizontal stabilizer off as they were jettisoned from the aircraft.

This happened at least once to another F-105 during my tour. There was a "caution note" in the Operating Manual to jettison the fuel tanks only during an unloaded straight and level flight condition, and not above 350 Kts. I debated only a moment or two, but knew I could not slow down nor stop jinking. So I thought, "screw the restriction, I'll jettison the tanks." I felt I had no choice.

I was in a turn, pulling Gs, and indicating about 580 Kts, pushing Mach 1 at about 12,000 ft. I reached for the red "tanks jettison" button, hesitated a second to prepare myself for what might happen next, and pushed it. I felt the aircraft jump up as it lightened, and accelerate even more, and within a second or two, I knew the tanks had cleared the stabilizer,..I was O.K.

I remembered I was still on rescue frequency, Ch 14 and not on Guard frequency and that I had better transmit my situation on Guard. I did, and then returned back to Ch 14 and monitored Guard frequency.

Two beepers were still screeching on guard frequency and I could hear Tomahawk 1 still trying to vector the Sandies into a position so they could make visual contact with Carbine 3 on the ground. Carbine 1 was trying to talk to Crown and also establish contact with us as he was entering the area to relieve us in the rescap effort. Now the frequencies were really jammed with chatter and Carbines screeching beepers.

I had just been hit by a Mig's missile and was trying desperately to let someone know what had happened. I was still trying to disengage the Migs who were pursuing us. They were hungry for the taste of another F-105 Yankee kill, and I couldn't get a word in edgewise. Things were turning sour and sounding very bad for any success of a rescue and my survival as well.

When I looked at the airspeed tape, I was supersonic, 1.05 mach, and accelerating. Then I looked at the fuel gage. I only had 2500 lbs remaining. I was shocked, but shouldn't have been, considering how long I'd been in burner and as little fuel as I had left when I was tapped by the Migs. I came out of burner to save enough gas to allow me to rendezvous with a tanker for refueling, but I still had to shake these Migs. I felt like I was in a catch 22. I didn't have any good choices left. I could run out of fuel by staying at this high power setting which would ensure keeping my speed up to avoid getting shot down, or if I'm lucky, I can stretch the fuel, take my chances on evading the Migs with less speed, and maybe I'll have enough fuel to get to a tanker, if I can find one. I decided to take my chances and conserve fuel!

I felt Joe probably did not stay with me on the escape maneuver into the clouds. I was accelerating and jinking with some high "G" turns, but I really didn't have any choice. I remember checking with Joe at least twice to see if he was O.K. and if he still had me in sight. I was trying to keep some sort of flight integrity. He responded each time that he did, and for me to keep going. He sounded confident in his response, as though he was more concerned about me than himself.

I'd been in the clouds for about 45 seconds, sort of skimming the tops, but not too deep in them, when I decided to pop up and take a look to see if the Migs were still behind me or if I could rejoin as an element with Joe. I popped up above the clouds, skimming just the tops of the puffs so I could see in back of me, at 6 o'clock. At this point, I heard in my headset what sounded like someone saying "son-of-bitch", (The "Longest Mission" chapter in "Thud Ridge indicates that I said this after being hit). I probably said some worse things when that happened, but that was not with the mike button depressed. Actually, this transmission took place about a minute after I was hit.

This is what I remember happening. Joe Abbott (Tomahawk 4) got hit with the second Mig 21 missile during my ensuing engagement and escape maneuvering. The escape maneuvering lasted only about a minute. During that time, one of the Mig's was able to launch another missile at Joe who was trailing me, and when he got hit, I believe he transmitted, **"Oh, I'm Hit"** (which sounded very similar to "son-of-a-bitch" on the UHF frequency tape). To my knowledge, I never made the transmission.

In any event, almost simultaneously with this garbled transmission, and as I looked to my right and behind, in a slight right turn, I saw a plum of fire which at first looked like another missile being fired at me from one of the Mig 21's. I immediately increased my angle of bank and Gs as hard as I could.

I believed, at that point, that another missile was being fired at me. Then, as I continued to concentrate on the object, I started to see the plum getting bigger and bigger with a huge fire ball and pieces falling out of the fire ball. I then realized that this was not a missile, but an aircraft being shot down. My heart sunk! I knew it had to be either a Mig or Joe's F-105. I was almost afraid to ask for a check in. I banked back left to keep an eye on the flaming wreckage which was falling into the cloud deck below and to the ground. I then saw a chute blossom from out of nowhere, just above the cloud deck. I asked for Tomahawk 4 to check in, and waited, with no response. I called again, but no response. I then knew it had to be Joe's F-105 (Tomahawk 4) I was watching going down in flames.

The UHF radio was now filled and saturated with a new sound. Triple beepers, were now screeching. Two from Carbine 3, and 4, and a new one from Tomahawk 4, Joe's parachute beeper, as he floated down into the clouds and the jungle below. About this time, I was on UHF channel 14 still trying to call someone. I really didn't care who I talked to. I just wanted to notify someone of our new problem. I called Cleveland flight who was entering the area and said, "Cleveland-this is Tomahawk 3. I'm headed out, low on fuel and in burner and there's Twenty-ones in the area. I've been hit and am 66 miles north of Ch 97 and I think they just shot down Tomahawk 4." I did not want to clutter the radio frequency since the rescue effort for Carbine 3 was still going strong, but I had to let someone know we had another F-105 pilot down, and I really thought I would be next.

At this point, the intercom of Carbine one's tape-recorder reflects the frustration after this call. Ben Fuller (Carbine Lead) says "Oh, man, not another one! Norm Frith (His Bear) says simply, "Ohhhhh."

Tomahawk 1 and 2 had started up from providing cover for Carbine 3 once they heard we were engaged by Mig 21s. They were flying south to assist me and Tomahawk 4 when the Mig 21's second missile hit Joe's F-105. Tomahawk 1 saw Tomahawk 4's chute and the aircraft debris falling down. Tomahawk 1 & 2 were also low on fuel by now but gave assistance and reassurance to 4 that rescue would be on the way and for him to turn his beeper off.

My contact with Tomahawk 1 was to ask him if he had 4 in sight and to tell him I was leaving the area because I was low on fuel, hit, and must leave to find a tanker and hope I could make it. Lead agrees and continued to assist Tomahawk 4 who is now on the ground.

While this is all going on, Carbine 1 who had just entered the rescue area again, had assumed control of the rescue effort for Carbine 3. He was now, still trying to get the Sandies to find Carbine 3 on the ground so the helicopters could be called in for the rescue.

Tomahawk 1 was trying to pinpoint Tomahawk 4 and also coordinate some sort of rescue effort for him. I remember exiting the area, listening to all this, and hearing the last of the transmissions on guard from Carbine 3 on the ground. Someone (I think Carbine 1, Ben) keeps saying "Turn the beeper off, Turn the beeper off".

About this time, I established contact with Crown and relayed to them that there are Migs in the area, that I'd been hit, and that I thought Migs also shot down another F-105, Tomahawk 4.

At that point I heard this transmission, " Tomahawk, Tomahawk, where are you?"

I didn't answer! I couldn't! I thought, no one seems to know what's going on except what's left of Carbine and Tomahawk flight, and that wasn't much.

I was still picking up the transmissions from Carbine as I continued south to channel 97 and hopefully a tanker. Finally I heard Crown tell Carbine 1 that they will have to clear the Migs out of the area before the helicopters can be cleared in for the rescue. A frustrated Carbine 1 told Crown that the Migs are between them and Ch 97, and there were no Migs in the rescue area. Carbine 1 was still trying to get the Helicopters in with no luck. By now, Carbine 1 & 2 were running low on fuel too.

Finally the Sandies were informed to bring the helicopters in when they were ready, but there was no response! Some more transmissions were heard from Carbine to the Sandies, and to Crown and back and forth and finally a desperate, sickening transmission is heard as I continued south toward CH 97 and hopefully a tanker! It was kind of muffled and squeaky,

*Major Leo Thorsness*

*Colonel Ben Fuller*

*Major Norman Frith*

coming from the hand held survival radio of Carbine 3, Leo Thorsness, on guard frequency.

Leo (Carbine 3) was making one more desperate plea on guard frequency to anyone who could hear it. He said, "They're coming up the hill after us— Get me out of here! Get me out of here! **Get me out of here!**".

I broke down and cried!

On intercom, Carbine 1's Bear (Norm Frith) says, "What did he say?" Carbine 1, front seater (Ben Fuller) says , in sort of a very low, quiet tone, which reflects the attitude of how much he hated to repeat the words. *"He said get me out of here".* Then silence.

We never did get them out! They spent almost 6 years in the Hanoi Hilton but the good news is that they all came out with the POWs in '73.

# Chapter Eight
# *Failed Rescue Aftermath*

With the rescue effort now expanding to getting Tomahawk 4, Joe Abbott out also, it was becoming painfully obvious that the rescue effort for Carbine 3 would be more difficult. Leo's last desperate plea for us to get him out, spurred the rescue effort to a new high. We weren't about to give up yet. There was still that slim chance that we could get all the guys out, Leo, Harry, and Tomahawk 4, Joe Abbott. But that was not to be.

Waco flight (Col Broughton) came back in the area and took over the rescue effort for Carbine 3 & 4 and Tomahawk 4. He pinpointed Tomahawk 4's position for the Sandies. The Choppers were called in but somehow on their way in, one of the choppers developed a mechanical problem and aborted, so the other chopper aborted with him, and they (Crown), called the rescue mission off.

This was about as much as you could take for one day, but there was one more episode still to occur that really made our day.

As the Sandies and helicopters were exiting the area, we heard, "Mayday, Mayday, Mayday,—Nomad (A-1, Sandy Lead) is hit and on fire". Within a few seconds, we heard another transmission. "Nomad—this is Nomad four, You're on fire, Bail out, bail out, **BAIL OUT!** There was a long pause. Then, "Bail out, you're on fire." Nomad Lead came back with, "Negative".

He wasn't about to bail out and risk getting rescued after what he had just witnessed. He knew what had already happened to the rescue attempt for Carbine 3, 4 and Tomahawk 4.

Instead, the damaged Sandy went to full throttle and by diving the A-1 to gain as much airspeed as he could, finally blew out the flames. (He made it back to Udorn where I talked to him later about the entire incident).

While this was going on, I was struggling to get organized myself, and recover from my engagement with the Mig 21's. After listening to the beepers, to Leo and Harry on the ground who were pleading to be rescued, all the chatter from the primary and guard frequencies, Joe (Tomahawk 4) just being shot down, and the thought that the Migs were still after my hide, I started to really feel sick to my stomach.

I started to cry, and couldn't stop. I knew I had to regain my composure, and make it to a tanker if I wanted to get this SOB on the ground safely and survive!

Then, I started to feel mad and angry at this whole mess. I seemed to regain some sort of confidence and strength. It was like being shot with some sort of adrenalin. Now, all of a sudden, I was bound and determined to make it. This transpired over a period of about 60 seconds or so, as I recall. I went from down in the dumps (literally), to on top of the world in just a few seconds, and all of a sudden I was convinced I'd make it. It was a weird feeling! The mind does funny things!

I climbed for altitude to conserve fuel, contacted the Radar control site (call sign "Brigham"), asked for vectors to the closest tanker, and declared an emergency. I only had about 500 lbs of fuel (5 mins, maybe) left on the gage, and was climbing in Military power when I decided to throttle back to a cruise setting and conserve what fuel I had left.

Brigham told me a tanker was on the way north, at about 25 miles port and asked, "Did I want the tanker to continue north?" I said, "hell no, turn him south". There was no way I was going to chase a tanker north. I figured, I wanted to be headed as far south as I could when I flame out, glide as far as I could, and then punch out as close to the Thai border as I could to help any rescue effort that I might need. At this point, I thought they would need all the help they could get. I had pretty much made up my mind to resolve myself of the worst situation, and that was ejection, but hopefully rescue.

As the fuel gage fluctuated, I was beginning to realize I wouldn't make the rendezvous with the tanker before I ran out of gas. I looked at the radar scope for a target, and sure enough, I had a large blip at about 20 degrees port at about 20 miles and it was really large. Brigham transmitted the tanker's position to be 20 miles, with a flight of 4 F-105's on it which were being refueled.

The tanker was at 26,000', heading north, and at first I really did not pay attention to the altitude so I stayed at about 35,000' looking level. It was hazy and a cirrus cloud deck between the tanker and me at about 30,000'. It took several sweeps on my radar to pick the tanker up. He only appeared on the bottom sweep (right to left).

That's when I realized that I was about 10,000 ft. above the tanker. I told Brigham to turn the tanker south. (Normal turn point was 22 miles at 20 degrees). We were in a perfect set up except I was way high and above the cirrus deck and couldn't get a visual on the tanker. I throttled back, descended and broke out of the clouds at about 28,000 ft. What a beautiful site! At about 10 degrees port and 10 miles was a tanker with 4 thuds on it. My thought was that I still had a chance with my overtake speed. My fuel gage indicated 200-to 0 lbs, on the digital markings. When you're that low, you really don't know what you have. I immediately asked for a tanker frequency. I switched and established contact with the tanker, and the thuds, and then made one transmission.

"This is Tomahawk 3, I'm out of gas,....been hit. 105's on the tanker ....get off, I need gas now!"

The Thuds on the tanker's wing immediately backed off to see what was happening. The thud on the boom came off! Fuel sprayed! It exited the boom at the disconnect, and the F-105 quickly moved to a wing position along with the rest of the flight.

It happened very quick. I never slowed down! I slipped into the engage position and plugged in to the tanker's boom without a word said. It was like magic, the quickest hook-up I have ever made with the least words being spoken. God, I was elated and happy! When I started to take on gas and the Thud kept running, I started to get hysterical! Laughing and crying, at the same time! I watched the fuel gage increase and you cannot believe the feeling of relief when something happens like this. When you're that close to losing it. When you're facing a survival situation which involves ejection, rescue, death, or worse—POW status- and now, you know that won't happen. You saved yourself,......Wow! What a great feeling!

I took on about 7 or 8 thousand pounds of fuel, enough to get to the closest AF Base, Udorn AB. I felt I needed to get this bird on the ground as soon as possible so whatever damage I received wouldn't develop into a more serious problem. I really didn't have a good indication of what was wrong. All I knew at the time was that I'd been hit by an air-to-air missile, some Yellow caution and Red warning lights came on and the gear horn was blowing. I remember some other red lights on too, but at the time, I couldn't pay close attention to them except to punch off the Master caution (Yellow) and Master warning (Red) lights. I was too busy trying to disengage the Mig 21's that were after us and provide some mutual support for Tomahawk 4 (Joe) to keep him from being shot down too.

After I refueled, I thanked the tanker and the flight of Thuds for their help and headed to Udorn. My Tacan/Nav equipment was out, so I notified Brigham radar control that I had battle damage and needed radar vectors to Udorn for a quick recovery. I then added that I thought it would be a good idea to have fire trucks standing by.

Brigham really did a great job of recovering me with some encouraging words. They were very calm and professional. I was impressed and felt that if anything happened while under their control, I was in good hands.

I kept looking back at my 6 o'clock for Migs even though I was deep in Laos by now and almost at Udorn, but I was really punchy at this point and didn't trust anyone or anything.

I landed at Udorn without any problems, so on rollout, I began to rejoice. The realization that I was down safely was more than I could stand. All that adrenalin was still working. I couldn't wait to park and get out of that F-105. A "Follow Me" truck met me at the end of the runway along with fire trucks that led me to the parking area away from the main ramp area. Blue vehicles were waiting with the intelligence guys for my quick transportation back to debriefing headquarters. I knew they had advanced notice of what had happened, the losses, and the unsuccessful rescue effort. They had a prize pilot to debrief and I was ready to pour my guts out to them, except I was tired as hell.

As I climbed out of the cockpit,—for me, it was a moment I wanted to cherish. I had made it back after all that had happened. I'd been hit, had to leave behind my wingman—somewhere in the jungle—now surviving, I hoped, and Carbine 3 and Bear were probably captured by now. At this time, I still was not aware that Carbine 4 was also shot down and still out there somewhere. That was the unaccounted for beeper we couldn't get turned off throughout the rescue effort. At this point, only Carbine 1 & 2 knew Carbine 4's fate and until they landed at Takhli and debriefed no one else at Takhli knew it. The whole thing was a mess!

I was soak and wet as I took off my parachute at the bottom of the ladder of my damaged F-105. I looked like a drowned rat, frazzled, blood shot eyes, wide open as they were from being scared for so long, I think. A crowd of officers and maintenance guys all introduced themselves and were looking at me in a very peculiar way, stunned at the way I looked (they later told me). I was taken to the Recce Hdqs and debriefing room and was told to relax and have a drink as they placed a bottle of "Old Something" whiskey in front of me and a paper cup. Later, the Flight Surgeon showed up and gave me some pills to take. I don't know what they were nor did I care.

I debriefed the entire episode with them as best as I could remember, in every detail. I answered a lot of questions they had, but they didn't seem to understand how this could happen. They were extremely interested in the Mig attack on me. At the time, I still did not know what had knocked down Carbine 3 nor did I know that we had lost Carbine 4. They wanted to know what shot them down, and I was only guessing that it was either ground fire or Migs, because no SAMs had been fired.

The Migs were getting smarter and bolder in their tactics. The intelligence people knew it, and I believe 7th Air Force was beginning to realize we could not continue ignoring the Mig threat as though it wasn't there. 7th AF was also anxious to learn about the failed rescue effort that should have been successful but wasn't. They wanted to know why not, and so did I! In addition, they had to be concerned about the tremendous loss we took, 3 F-105's and 4 pilots (on one mission) and we didn't even get to the target. When they heard about the Mig 21's being involved, that got their attention. I could tell from the interest and questions asked, that someone up the line wanted details. It appeared to me they were really concerned! I was glad!

After debriefing, I was told that a T-39 would be in the next day to pick me up and fly me back to Takhli. My F-105 would stay at Udorn for an inspection and maintenance. I would spend the night at Udorn and bunk with one of the Sandy pilot's. I was invited to the O'Club for dinner and drinks with the Udorn pilots (RF-101, A-1 and Helicopter), and that suited me fine. I couldn't "buy" a drink because drinks were flowing to me one after the other—on the house. We drank and talked till wee hours in the morning and I was feeling no pain by the time I made it back to the hooch where I spent the night.

The next morning I was on my way back to Takhli on a T-39. I was told that the Takhli force was launched into pack 6 on the morning mission for a Mig hunt and that rescue efforts for Carbine 3 & 4 and Tomahawk 4 at first light by the Sandies were unsuccessful because of a low cloud layer in the area. Encouraging was that they picked up the personal beepers of Tomahawk 4, but the bad news was that they did not raise Carbine 3 and 4. Rescue was rescheduled for the afternoon when the weather was suppose to improve.

Another attempt was made that afternoon but was unsuccessful. For weeks, everyone attempted to contact Tomahawk 4 in that area, but all efforts were unsuccessful. Joe Abbott (Tomahawk 4) was finally listed as MIA and later confirmed as a POW along with Leo, Harry, and Bob Abbott.

After arriving at Takhli, I debriefed with Col Broughton. We met in the Wing battle staff briefing room and when he arrived, he walked directly at me, extended his hand, smiled, gave me a firm friendly hand shake and said, " Welcome back Al, I'm glad you're back safe".

He wanted to know what happened to Joe and me and how we were engaged by the Migs and how Joe got shot down etc., I debriefed him on the mission. I remember as I recounted the experience again, I began to get excited, and my palms got sweaty, voice a little shaky but I managed to get through describing the whole episode to him from my view. After relating the experience, Col Broughton thanked me for hanging in there as long as I did during the rescap effort, particularly at 15,000 feet, 30 miles from Hanoi over the Red River. He then told me that the rescue efforts would continue until we can confirm their status. He also told me that it was determined that <u>Migs</u> had shot down Carbine 3 & 4, not ground fire. That was the first I'd heard that Carbine 4 had also been shot down.

To say the least, the talk I had with Col. Broughton made me feel better about myself and helped my self confidence which had been badly shaken. I was feeling very low by then but that little episode made me feel a lot better. Col Broughton went to the top of my list.

This mission and the previous pack 6 mission had really taken its toll on me. I only had 34 total missions and two to route pack 6. I had been through a lot in just a couple of pack 6 missions and it seemed as though I hadn't even started yet to fly the real tough ones I'd heard about in route pack 6. I felt snake bit! I had a long way to go.

# Chapter Nine
# MuGia Pass
## One Stinking Rail Car-1802/10550 — 8 May, '67

On 8 May, my 39th mission was fragged into route pack 1, MuGia Pass with a flight of 4 F-105s. Maj Bob Rilling was lead, Capt Dave Cobb was #2, I was #3 and Capt Mike McCuistion was # 4. I was Mike's Flight Commander at this time and he was fairly new in the Squadron. I think he only had about 15 missions or so. Mike had been Tomahawk 2 with me in the unsuccessful rescue mission near Hanoi a couple days earlier. The unfortunate part of this story is that Mike was scheduled for "Leave" and had planned to visit his wife on an extended R&R/Leave to Hawaii I believe. He was filling in on this mission because of a shortage of pilots, but instead of going on Leave the next day, he wound up being shot down and spending the next six years as a POW.

The entire Wing was feeling the pinch on the lack of pilots, and our Squadron (333 TFS) was particularly short during this flying period. We were loosing a lot of guys to combat in addition to the normal attrition of those experienced pilots who were completing their tours. New pilots were arriving, but we didn't have enough lower route pack sorties allocated to train them before turning them loose to pack 6. Things were heating up on the number of missions being flown into pack 6, and although pack 6 missions were always scheduled twice a day, they were not always flown because of weather. But now, we were being executed on them daily as the weather improved in the Hanoi target area.

It was our Flights primary week to fly the Squadron's allocated missions, and as his flight commander, I needed Mike M to fill a slot on this mission. I talked him into flying and to delay his leave for one day. Besides, it was to the lower route packs and this mission should be a piece of cake. Mike agreed and stayed to fly the mission.

We were a flight of four and all went well flying to the target area for our Route Recce mission. The flight lead, Bob Rilling, started to recce MuGia Pass. Unexpectedly, Lead called and said he spotted a single railroad car on the tracks between a ravine in the middle of the Pass. A perfect set up for a flak trap.

He immediately made a decision to make a run at it. He gave the bomb run line up order for roll in as 1,2,3,4. I was surprised at the quick decision, and I didn't really have the target in sight since I was flying his wing as element lead, number 3. I quickly slid out for a look and sure enough, I picked up a single box car on the railroad track at about the 2 o'clock position. I had an unpleasant feeling since we had been warned against this sort of target (single truck or rail car) as a possible flak trap. It was a very simple set up, get us to attack a worthless target with four F-105's and the odds are they will hammer at least one of us. One stinking railcar in exchange for at least one and maybe more F-105's, with pilots.

Prior experience led to a very sound policy in the Wing. Don't risk four F-

105's' and expend 24 (6X4 750 lb) bombs on one rail car unless your damn sure it's a lucrative target worth the price. It made sense to me. I didn't have a chance to respond or question the flight lead's decision before he started his roll in for the bomb run. We were committed! We needed to keep flight integrity so we made our runs in order, 1, 2, 3, 4. Mike was the last one in. As I came off the target, I looked back in a jink maneuver (hard left turn) to see the effects of my bomb drop and to pick up my wingman, Mike.

I saw tracers forming a fine (red) line and a very quick flash came off Mike's aircraft as he bottomed out of his run on the rail car. Mike had been hit as he pulled off the target. A few seconds later he called to say he was hit.

The entire flight reacted! I kept a visual on Mike and started to turn toward him and climb. Bob Rilling and Dave Cobb started to turn back for a join up also.

I could see Mike's aircraft starting to flash at the aft end. I told him to turn right toward the water, but Mike was continuing a left turn toward the west. During our mission briefing, we covered the safe bail out areas and reviewed the rescue procedures in case one of us was hit and forced to eject. We all knew the safest bail out area would be over the water if we made an attack in this area. We had briefed to make a run from south to north (if we could) with a break and jinking maneuver to the right toward the gulf, in case one of us was hit and needed to bail out for rescue.

All of us in the flight continued to transmit to Mike to turn right, (east), to get over the water, but to no avail. His aircraft began to burn more furiously from the rear, near the horizontal stabilizer, the speed brake area at the tail end. He was climbing and turning west, more inland. Things were not looking good for Mike. We were all transmitting and shouting at Mike to "Turn right" but I believe he either didn't hear us or his controls were giving him fits to the point that he couldn't concentrate on what we were saying. He had to be in a panic, his engine fire light must have been on! He was burning bad from the rear end, and it was getting worse.

We all followed him trying to keep him advised of the status of the aircraft and the fire as best we could. This lasted for only about 45 seconds but it seemed like an eternity. Finally the fire got so bad, it looked like the aircraft was getting engulfed in flames and ready to blow up, at which point I finally blurted, "Get Out, Bail Out". It was instinctive.

We repeated the instructions for Mike to Bail Out several times for about 15 seconds. Mike never made a transmission from the time he said he had been hit.

I suspect his radio went out and he never received our transmissions nor could he transmit.

Then the canopy ejected with a flash, rising high above the burning aircraft, followed very quickly by Mike in the ejection seat. Immediately, the aircraft went into a left descending spiral, burning like hell, and coming apart, falling in pieces, the tail separating and burning in a mass of falling metal from the tail end. Mike's ejection seat came up and out of the F-105 clean. Mike separated from the seat, the chute blossomed and began to float to the ground from about 4 or 5 thousand feet. The gooks were waiting for him and we knew it!

Lead, (Rilling) told me to go high, get the coordinates and provide radio relay. Again, I was put in the same role as I had been in before as high rescap cover and radio relay. No big deal, but the same thoughts went through my mind, and I also realized that Mike was also part of that unsuccessful rescue a couple days ago too. I wondered what he was thinking!

I climbed to an altitude that gave me the TACAN reception of channel # 89, Nakom-Phenom (NKP). That Air base not only had a TACAN station, but also the Rescue aircraft, Sandies, and Choppers. In this case, the TACAN made a good reference for updating the doppler Navigation system which helped pinpoint the downed crewmember. I had to fly closer toward the TACAN station to get a good reliable fix. Then I gave the range and bearing from CH 89 to Crown and they acknowledged the position. Maj Rilling established contact with Crown and relayed our situation and requested the rescue effort.

As we waited for the Sandies and Choppers, time was beginning to run out. Mike was talking to us on his hand held personal emergency radio (Guard). He was concerned. I guess so! Gooks were coming up the small hill he was on and getting closer every minute. Rilling and Dave Cobb were making strafing runs on the Viet Cong who were trying to get to Mike. They made pass after pass, trying to keep them away and help sanitize the area for the Sandies and Choppers. I could see the action from my position further to the west -southwest, where I was able to establish radio contact with Crown, and give a good range and bearing to the rescue area.

We were already past our minimum fuel to return to Takhli without refueling so I arranged for a tanker to rendezvous with us. This would allow us either to come back to the rescue area for support or return to base. About this time, a Weasel flight in the area had heard us on Guard and offered assistance. I gave them the range and bearing from Ch 89 and they were on their way in to take our place while we refueled. Soon the Sandies contacted us. They were approaching the area and needed vectors to Mike.

Things were looking good for the rescue. Mike's chute was still spread out and visible on the ground, just like the rescue guys and procedures called for. Mike was doing everything right. Staying in radio contact, displaying his chute, and staying as calm as he could under the circumstances. The Sandies finally spotted the chute on the ground and began to sanitize the area. At this point, they took control of the rescue effort and began coordinating with Crown, the rescue coordinator. The Weasels came into the area and were standing by to lend assistance. We were now out of the picture and low on fuel, so we joined up and proceeded to a tanker.

As we proceeded out of the area to the tanker, we monitored the rescue effort on Guard and began to realize they were having problems getting approval for the Choppers to go in for the rescue.

Crown told the Sandies that they did not have the required General Officer's approval yet to clear the Choppers in. (First the Sandies had to sanitize the area and request the Choppers to come in for the pick up. Crown would then request the authority to send the Choppers in). The Sandies had sanitized the area and requested the Choppers but they were lacking the clearance authority! The Viet Cong were proceeding up the hill after Mike and he didn't have much time left. Still, Crown insisted that they needed clearance from a Flag/

General Officer before Choppers could be sent in. This was becoming ridiculous!

We were frustrated, listening to what was happening, when out of no where, "Mother Goose" called, (A Navy rescue Chopper) who offered assistance. I couldn't believe what I was hearing. Mike must be lucky. The Navy to the rescue? Thank the Lord! Someone has some sense in this mixed up war. They said they would come in an pick up the downed crew, and had asked no questions about authority. The Sandies accepted their offer.

They started in, from about 40 miles out, from their station off the coast. They were inbound, and we were elated. It didn't take long, maybe about one or two minutes, when the Sandies made a panic call on Guard. They watched Mike's parachute being gathered up by several people (Viet Cong). They tried to establish contact with Mike on Guard, but received no answer. They tried repeatedly to contact Mike, but got no response.

Soon, the Sandies said they did not have the downed pilot in sight anymore. Very shortly after that, Crown contacted us while we were on the tanker to tell us the rescue effort was terminated and it looked like the pilot was captured. We were being released to return to Takhli.

I was depressed, to say the least. I took it pretty hard because this was the second rescue mission I was on and both had failed. This one had a unique twist. Mike was in my Flight, and I had asked him to cancel his leave to fly this, so called, easy mission to route pack 1. I did not envision this mission turning into his last. We returned to Takhli, without Mike. I lived with that for a long time, still do, because Mike spent 6 years in the Hanoi Hilton as a result.

# Chapter Ten
# Migs & More Migs
## May 20, '67: Mission #48
## Bac Le RR Siding, 2131/10626 (Northeast RR)

Four Mig's were destroyed during the afternoon of 20 May 1967 by two flights of F-4s from the 8th TFW, Ubon, who flew MIGCAP for the Takhli (355th) F-105 strike force mission against the Bac Le railroad yards on the NE railroad, northeast of Hanoi in pack 6. I was element lead (number 3) in one of the F-105 flights in the strike force.

The weather had turned bad in pack 6 a couple of weeks prior to this mission with thunderstorms and pack 6 targets socked in with weather. I also had a 5 day R&R prior to this mission so I had a reprieve from pack 6 targets until my 48th. This was my 4th pack 6 mission and 2nd to the northeast railroad and all had been very stressing and full of bad experiences. I would learn to hate the NE railroad targets and this is the one that helped formulate that attitude which lasted the rest of my tour.

Each of my previous pack 6 missions had resulted in losses to the force and friends I knew. I didn't expect flying these missions would get to me as much as I felt they would. The last "Pack 6" mission to Bac Ninh RR bridge on the NE railroad wasn't to bad but losing Mike McCuistion the way we did in MuGia Pass (Pack 1) didn't help my attitude. This mission would be another one that contributed to my deteriorating confidence, break down, and eventual hospitalization for a rest.

After several early morning missions, I began seeing the Flight Surgeon to get some sleeping pills since I couldn't sleep at night. Briefings were at 3:30 A.M.for the early morning missions to pack 6 targets. I would try to get enough sleep by going to bed by 9 P.M. but that didn't work very well. Most of the time I couldn't fall asleep until midnight, thinking about the mission. So I would ask the Flight Surgeon for sleeping pills to help me sleep. He gave me sleeping pills and told me to take them an hour before going to bed, which I did.

He detected something in my behavior after this mission (he called it "battle fatigue") and decided to monitor me for a while. Six days and 2 missions later, on the next pack 6 mission, I lost my roommate (Capt Gordon "Buz" Blackwood) and as a result, the Flight Surgeon recommended I rest for a couple days in the hospital. That suited me fine because I sensed losing all confidence in myself, confused and afraid to go back to pack 6, particularly to the NE railroad targets. I didn't know what was happening to me. I felt I was really losing it!

The Northeast railroad was the most heavily defended transportation route in North Vietnam since it was their main railroad supply route from China through Hanoi and further south to South Vietnam. Supplies and equipment were shipped South for troops fighting in the southern parts of North and South Vietnam. All along the railroad were sidings, and of course, defenses, Flak sites, SAMs and several airfields in close proximity to the railroad.

This, and all other trans-shipment routes seemed to be our primary targets. It made sense to take them out, but it seemed that's all we did. We were restricted from hitting any dams or airfields during this time which would have devastated the area. Very strict rules and restrictions were put on the Air Force which prevented us from striking these targets.

Every target was personally selected at the highest levels in the U.S. Government. The President and his cabinet members approved and directed the targets to be struck, daily. At our level, they were referred to and labeled "Joint Chiefs of Staff (JCS)" targets. A very bad way to fight a war, if you're fighting to win. It didn't take a genius to know we weren't going to win by only bombing these targets. We were getting eaten alive by more and more flak sites around these type targets. More Migs were attacking us because they knew we were not going to bomb their airfields. They were off limits by our own restrictions. SAM sites were cropping up all over North Vietnam and were being put on mobile trailers for changing location daily. It became frustrating as hell!

This particular mission is highlighted in the Aces & Aerial Victories (The United States Air Force in Southeast Asia 1965-1973, Chapter II, Combat Narratives: 1965-1968 by Charles A. Ravenstein, published by the Office of Air Force History Headquarters USAF, 1976. The episode in that Chapter is titled "An Old-Fashioned Dogfight"). It captures the F-4 Mig Cap flight's aggressive dogfight with 8 F-4's battling 12 to 14 Mig-17's while we (F-105 strike force) proceeded to the target. Col. Olds/Steve Croker, John Pardo/Steve Wayne, Phil Combies/Dan Lafferty were credited with Mig kills during that mission.

The F-105 strike force from Takhli consisted of 5 flights of F-105's (Weasel flight, Flak suppression

Col. Olds, the first quadruple MIG-killer of the Vietnam War, prepares to nail four more red stars to the 8th TFW scoreboard. Other victors in the 20 May encounter (L to R) are: Maj. Combies, Lt. Lafferty, Maj. Pardo, and Lts. Croker and Wayne (front center).

flight, and 3 bomb flights) attacking the JCS target, Bac Le railroad yard, on the NE railroad just north of Kep. We had to use Brown anchor tankers, located just east of Hue in the Gulf, north of the 17th parallel. The Ubon 8th TFW guys (Col. Olds & Company) in their F-4's were flying Mig Cap for us. We would rendezvous with them as we dropped off the tankers around the 19th parallel and head north to pack 6 over the gulf.

I must say here, that having the F-4 Mig Cap meant an awful lot to us F-105 guys as we went into pack 6. They did one hell of a good job keeping the Migs off of us so we could get to the target without having to dump our bombs to protect ourselves against Migs when they attacked us on ingress. We (F-105's) were no match for them in air-to-air dog fighting. The Migs had the turning advantage, but we had the speed advantage. It was not considered smart to get into a turning, fighting contest with a Mig 17 or 21. Our best tactic was speed, hit and run, but don't get into a dog fight, turning contest.

This was an afternoon mission and briefings went normal. The force was scheduled to take off around 1 P.M. Our flight consisted of Bob Rilling, lead, Dave Cobb #2, me #3 and 1/Lt Mathews number 4. Mathews and I roomed together in the same hooch until he finished his 100 missions, and then finally left with a completed tour.

The start, taxi, Takeoff, and rendezvous with the tankers at Brown anchor, off the gulf coast, east of Dong Hoi and Hue, were routine. As usual, the ingress to the "Ile Madeleine", our turn point prior to entering pack 6, was uneventful. The F-4 Mig Cap joined us at tanker drop off but this time they supported us with two flights of 4 instead of one. They positioned themselves so as to have one flight of four up front of the force and one flight behind, always high.

We "cleaned em up, and greened em up", and turned on the ECM pods (Music) as we dropped off the tankers. That is, we ran through the post refueling checklist of making sure we closed and locked the refueling door, retracted the leading edge slats and a few other clean-up items. Then "green up" the armament system. Arm the bombs, gun (with circuit breaker), missiles and make sure you had green lights on the armament panel for final assurance.

About 70 miles out from the turn point (Ile Madeleine") from the target, we started a descent from our cruise altitude (15,000') to about 500 feet over the water and Island turn point. We needed to get out of North Vietnam's SAM, Fire Control, and ground fighter Interceptor radar control coverage as we approached North Vietnam defenses.

We started down and I could see a lot of cloud build ups in front of us. We usually had some middle cloud build ups in this area (just off the coastal islands where our turn point was) which sometimes complicated our turn on course for our final run to the target.

I remember circumventing some of the build ups in the area before reaching the Island. I always worried about the cloud decks and not being able to see below or being trapped in between layers because of the SAM threat. We wanted to not be right on top of a cloud layer because their would be no room for evading a SAM when it popped through the under-cast if you were right on top of a deck of clouds. The rule was to fly at least a 1,000 feet above a cloud layer. It was assumed the North Vietnamese knew the altitude of the cloud tops. They used this information for setting the SAM fuses to detonate at that altitude if tracking failed.

It was about a 75 NM run in from the coast to the railroad. Our dead reckoning navigation was calculated in terms of minutes. Normally, for the run in from the IP, when entering pack 6, our speed was calculated for 9 mi/min. We'd plug in the burner after the turn point at the island, off the Gulf, and accelerate to 540 Kts (9 mi/min). The total amount of time for ingress and egress exposed us to about 20 minutes of heavy defenses in pack 6 (about 9 in and 11 out). Time was allowed for the pop maneuver, dive bomb run over the target, and 180 degree turn coming off the target and jinking on the way out for egress.

The critical time, or most vulnerable time for being shot down or taking battle damage was the last 3 minutes before the target, over the target (especially), and the first couple minutes of egress. The majority of the flak was concentrated in this area and over the target. Usually, the Migs would attack us before we got to the target to try to force us to drop our bombs. It was a well coordinated effort on their part because SAMs needed to be fired at us either before or after the Mig attacks or they might shoot down one of their own Mig aircraft.

The Migs would not follow us all the way into the target because of the flak over the target. They didn't want to get shot down by their own flak. So we could expect the most heaviest flak and SAM launches right in and around the target ( within a 5 to 10 mile radius). The Migs would attack outside that area on ingress to get us to abort the run and on egress to pick up a straggler and maybe a Yankee kill.

We were like sitting ducks as we started a slow climb for the pop up, slowing down a bit, hanging slightly to line ourselves up for the final bomb run. The next several seconds, during the bomb run is when we were the most vulnerable. We had to ignore the flak, SAMs and Migs for the next 30 to 60 seconds because this is what we had come all this way for and we didn't want to return for more of the same. We needed to destroy the target with good bombs or the trip was wasted.

On this mission, our flight was the last bomb flight in the strike force of 5 flights. As we approached the "Ile Madeleine" turn point, I could see the lead flight making his turn to the west over the island and the lead F-4 MigCap flight out in front. In the distance, I saw the F-105 Weasel flight already smoking west and could hear their SAM warnings starting to pick up.

Weasel Flight—"Their looking at us at 12 o'clock, 1 ringer, no threat to the force".

These warnings came more rapidly, and more intense from the weasel flight. As our flight turned inbound to the west toward the northeast railroad, and as the last flight in the string, we engaged the afterburners to stay up with the rest of the flights in front of us. We stayed in minimum burner, "en route" formation, which was just a loose fingertip formation. Our heads swiveling all the while, looking for Migs and SAMs.

We were about 1,000 ft, and level with the range of mountain peaks to the south which we used for masking. The ride was bumpy, and the moisture or humidity at these speeds caused clouds of vapor trails to engulf the airplane and streamers to come off the wing tips at the slightest G force or loading on the aircraft. You could see the 6 X 750lb bombs on the Multiple Ejection Rack (MER) of the wingmen bumping together from the rough ride. As long as the fuses on the bombs were still safetied with wire and the arming propeller wasn't turning, there wasn't much to worry about, but it looked dangerous as hell.

Things heated up quickly. About 2 or 3 minutes into the ingress, the Weasels started to pick up heavy SAM activity and were calling SAM warnings all over the place. I was picking up a lot of activity on my Radar-Homing -and -Warning (RHAW) gear also, but it usually was not considered reliable because of all the electronic emissions from our own ECM pods, the RB-66's and Radar Control Flak sites etc. At least it was not as reliable as the Weasel warning gear, so I turned my RHAW gear off. That eliminated the excess noise in my headset so I was more able to hear transmissions on strike frequency and Guard.

At this point, you don't want to miss any transmissions. We were also picking up Mig warnings from as far back as the turn point off the coast, so we knew Migs were also on the way to greet us.

All of a sudden, the Weasels called a 3 ring SAM warning and the Weasel leader sounded concerned. The pitch level of his voice increased and he became more panic sounding. Weasel Lead wasn't telling the force "no threat to the force" anymore. That got my attention! Then without warning, Lead Weasel transmitted "There looking at us"! They were getting ready to launch. He followed quickly by transmitting to his flight to pull it up and get ready to fire on his count. I looked to my left through our flight lead, since I was on the right wing, and picked up the Weasel flight pulling up in fingertip formation out ahead of us, about a mile.

Then I heard his count down start from 5, 4, 3 etc, and then, "Fire". It was like 4th of July! Shrike (AGM-45) missiles came off all four F-105's in a cloud of white exhaust smoke and fire from the rocket motors. The Shrikes were on their way to a SAM radar launch site. They (SAM radar) would either have to shut down their tracking radar or the Shrikes would home on the radar beam to the transmitting site and destroy it. The North Vietnamese usually shut down their radar site and let the SAM they had fired go unguided. When that happened, the Weasels had done their job of protecting us from the SAMs.

Shortly, SAMs came flying over us. We were not in a position to do anything in the way of evasive action to avoid them anyway. We were lucky! We kept pressing, in formation, in afterburner, going as fast as the burner would carry us and still stay in some sort of fingertip, "route formation", on the way to the target.

Almost simultaneously, I saw some Migs on our port side, about a mile or less, a Flight of two. They were Mig-17's. I quickly looked to my right also and saw some more Migs. I don't even remember what kind, but Migs were everywhere. All over the strike force. I didn't have time to do a lot of looking for Migs since we were in formation, doing about 550 Kts (.87 Mach) and it was bumpy as hell.

At the same time, about 3 minutes out, the first flight of F-4's sighted the

Mig's also and the F-4's came alive. They started to call Migs and chatter about preparations to engage them. (In the next 12 to 14 minutes, there was a massive and aggressive dogfight with 8 F-4's battling 12-14 Mig-17's. I later found out that Four Mig's were destroyed in a span of 5 to 6 minutes during this battle).

To my amazement, our leader called sighting Migs on our starboard side. Rilling quickly and without warning, jettisoned his bombs and said he was going after the Migs. Dave Cobb, #2 had no choice and was probably as confused as I, so he followed the leader. They broke "Up" and "Right" above me and disappeared.

I thought, "I came this far with a full load of bombs, and only 3 minutes from the target, and by God, I'm going to get 'Bombs on the target' like the frag said". I figured, the F-4's will take care of the Migs and that's their job. Our job was to destroy the target we were assigned. When lead and 2 peeled off to the right with no warning, I felt like a lost soul with a wingman. Within seconds, I realized I was a flight lead, responsible for leading #4 to the roll in point and into the dive bomb run. My adrenalin started to flow and I focused on the target in front of me, the pop up point, and the flights in front of us.

I couldn't believe that lead had left us so suddenly. The Migs were not a threat to us at that point and we were only a few minutes short of the target. I wasn't happy with the prospect that now my wingman and I were choice stragglers for Migs as a flight of 2 instead of 4.

The Mission called for the force to divide at the start of the pop maneuver and strike the target with the first flight of F-105's attacking from the south and the second flight of F-105's attacking from the north, the third from the South, the fourth from the North. We called it a "Butterfly Approach", where every other bomb flight would alternate the attack direction. The F-4's would escort us to the start of our climb for the roll in and then break off and wait for us on the way out unless they encounter Migs before that point.

I started a slight climb for the top of the bomb run striving for the right point that would give me a good 45 degree dive angle or better, for the run. Flak (black puffs) was going off all over us. Occasional fire balls were visible on the closer ones. Even as my concentration was on the target, I could not help but see the stuff going off around me in my peripheral vision. I finally rolled in, got the dive angle I wanted, checked the airspeed, shifted my eyes to the target and back to the pipper with a quick check of airspeed, angle, altitude, one more pipper check, adjust, and pickle the bombs off. This takes all of about 6 or 7 seconds, not long but it seems like an eternity. I really don't know how good the bomb damage was, but the bomb damage assessment from our bomb film back at Takhli showed significant damage to the rail yard, tracks and cars that were in the yard siding at the time.

We came off the target and I was scared as hell because flak was bursting all over me from the time we started the pop and it didn't let up. Mostly, grey stuff (57 MM) and a lot of black puffs higher up (85 MM) going off all over me and number 4. I could see the muzzle flashes during the dive bomb run from the flak sites. Flak sites ringed the entire area on both sides of the railroad tracks. Six to eight guns in a site, sort of in a circle, sequentially firing. Scary as hell! They were really homing in on us because we were the last flight in the force and they had plenty of practice by the time we rolled in and there were only 2 of us.

During this time, transmissions from the F-4's on the strike frequency, as they were fighting the Migs, were becoming irritating. Chatter from the F-105 flights in front of us trying to join up after the bomb run, Mig calls on Guard frequency from the Navy ship off shore, and the Weasels still trying to warn us of SAM threats, all made you want to turn the radio completely off, but you knew you couldn't if you wanted to survive. It was heated and confusing to say the least.

I came off the target and jinked left and right, Plugged in the burner to gain speed I'd lost in the dive bomb recovery, but I needed to keep my airspeed down so my wingman could join up. I was happy because I survived the bomb run (the most vulnerable time) and was on my way out. All I had to do now, was hang on for another 8 minutes for egress and I'd have another "mark" (Mission counter toward 100). But it wasn't over yet.

I no sooner came off the target, jinked a few times and looked back once to check my 6 o'clock for Mathews, my wingman, when I began to encounter numerous aircraft in front of me. The radio frequency was filled with the F-4 pilots screaming at each other in a heated Mig engagement. Someone was yelling, "Keep turning, keep turning, that's it, you've got him now, etc. etc." It was deafening!

Then, and this is what really upset me, I saw an aircraft in front of me and it looked like an F-105. It was burning, in a spiral, coming down with pieces falling off. I saw F-4s all around, some still engaged with Migs and I blasted right through them, quite unexpectedly. Bear in mind, my airspeed was about 500 kts and I was jinking at about 500 ft, when out of nowhere, I see this plane going down in flames, right in front of me. I looked for a chute but didn't see one. The plane kept going down in flames, breaking up and finally hitting the ground as I passed over head. I looked back in a jinking maneuver, but still didn't see a chute. I could see a mass gaggle of F-4s and Migs engaged in turning maneuvers but no chute. The airplane was burning on the ground. It exploded when it hit. One hell of a mess! Since I thought it was one of our F-105's, I noted the location for debriefing. I didn't hear a beeper, so I double checked that I had the Guard receiver on the "Receive" position. I did!

To this day, I would swear that it was a F-105 that went down. I thought, "God, they nailed one of our guys". All the way home I believed we lost someone. I was depressed as hell knowing we lost someone and trying to figure out who this might be and in what flight he belonged. I had about another hour and a half or two to think about it during the return flight to Takhli. As it turned out, we didn't lose anyone. The F-4's shot down four Migs and the aircraft I saw had to be one of them, but I didn't know it at the time.

My number 4, Mathews, had joined up after I witnessed the burning aircraft go down as I slowed down, came out of burner but still kept the speed up, slowly weaving, varying the altitude to complicate any gun tracking on us and still allow 4 to join up.

The F-4's were still cluttering the UHF strike frequency fighting the Migs, so I switched #4 to our discrete frequency so we could talk. We must have been about 3 minutes from the coast and about 1,000 feet with the mountain range to our right (South). I kept checking our 6 o'clock position for Migs. Mathews was trailing and falling behind on my right when I detected flak puffs bursting just behind him. A trail of grey and black puffs were following him so I told him they were shooting at him and that the flak was bursting just behind him. He called back and said his cabin heat had gone full hot and he was already at full military power but still loosing out. I was at a reduced power setting already and hated to slow down anymore since we were just staying in front of the flak bursts. I kept urging 4 to push it up and was afraid if he slowed down, he'd catch one of those 57's that were bursting just behind him.

We made it to the coast but just as we started to pass over the mainland and over some of the small islands, another barrage let loose at us, so I climbed and jinked and within about 30 seconds we were through the flak and over the gulf.

It was time to start heading south for our post strike refueling. We rendezvoused with the waiting tankers, joined, and took on our fuel for the rest of the journey back to Takhli. All the way back, I kept thinking about the F-105 I'd seen shot down, going down in flames. Mathews still had cabin heat problems off and on but managed to hang in there the rest of the trip. (He was soak and wet when he crawled out of the cockpit back at Takhli).

We were the last flight to land at Takhli and after I parked, Maj Jody Jones, one of the guys in our squadron, met me at the aircraft. It was custom for the guys not flying the mission to meet the ones coming back from pack 6 with a beer and welcome those who made it back with all the gusto you could, under the circumstances.

I remember this very distinctly. After I parked, I felt absolutely beat, in a daze. I opened the canopy and just sat there for a long time reflecting on the entire mission, the leader leaving us, Migs attacking, SAMs launched at us, flak over the target and all the way out. But the most important part that hurt me was watching the F-105 going down in flames, right in front of me, while listening to the F-4's battling the Migs. I was home safe, parked, and had one more day to live and one more mark counter toward the 100 mission criteria that would get me back home, if I was lucky.

"Jonesy" came up the ladder, and I remember him saying something like "welcome back Al, have a beer" as he extended the beer to me. I didn't even look at him nor take the beer. I was frozen in the cockpit, I just stared off into space unable to say anything, just staring. Jones said " I hear it was a tough mission, are you alright?" I nodded and said, "yeh, but we lost one." He said "no, everyone made it back".

He could see I was depressed as hell. I said "No, I saw an F-105 go down in flames in front of me." Jones tried to console me and kept insisting that we had not lost anyone. I couldn't believe what he was saying and I told him, "I know we lost a guy because I saw him go down."

It was like I wanted to stay in the cockpit now that I was on the ground and just relax. The feeling of being back, on the ramp and parked was such a happy time. Safe from anymore flak, SAMs and Migs but still in the cockpit. I was still dazed and somewhat incoherent because now things were not making sense to me. I was confused and drained!

Jones then tried to get me to relax. I kept telling him that we lost an F-105, by saying "I saw him go down in flames but no beeper." I kept repeating and insisting that I saw an F-105 get shot down, and he kept telling me that we didn't loose anyone. If nothing else, Jones got me out of the cockpit, down the ladder and into the van that met the returning pilots for transportation to the intelligence debriefing area in Wing Hdq.

I was in a state of shock. The adrenalin had worn off from the mission excitement, and I was in the let down period which could be a high or very low, depending on what you experienced on the mission. In this case I went into depression, a very "low" period. The bad experiences were piling up on me and this one didn't help.

I proceeded to debriefing and met with #4, Mathews. We greeted each other with a hand shake and talked about his heat going full hot and the flak eating him up and the Flight Lead leaving us just before reaching the target, laughing about a few things but really happy about being back alive. We sat down with the Intelligence debriefing officer. All the other flights had already debriefed the mission. The intelligence officer put a bottle of "Ole Turkey" whiskey in front of us and some paper cups. I poured a full cup of whiskey and took a long drink. Within minutes, the paper cup started to melt.

I recapped the mission as I saw it and insisted that I saw a F-105 shot down and the intelligence debriefer insisted that neither our strike force or Korat's lost an aircraft. They told me that the F-4's shot down 4 Migs and they didn't loose an aircraft either.

I was glad that I was wrong but that was the crowning blow for me. I was completely drained and confused. I thought I knew what I saw. An F-105 going down in flames. Now I'm being told, that was not true. We didn't loose an F-105! I began to think I was loosing my mind. I mean, I've never been more certain about something than this. Now I was beginning to doubt myself. Could I be wrong?

What I apparently saw was the Mig that one of the F-4's shot down as I was coming off the target. I must have flown right through the engagement. The account from the Air Force History Book chapter says—"There were eight F-4C's, twelve Mig-17's, and one odd flight of F-105's on their way out form the target, who flashed through the battle area." It had to be one of the Migs being shot down that I saw as I flew through that engagement. It sure looked like an F-105 to me at the time.

My confidence was going to hell in a hand basket. I felt I was cracking, badly!

I left debriefing feeling like, "I'll accept their version and hang in there. Maybe I'm wrong". But the funny part was that I was beginning to believe their version, which meant that what I saw was not what I thought I saw, and that scared me! I thought, to hell with it, I'm alive, and I still have the evening and this night to live before tomorrow's mission, so live it up.

I looked at the bomb damage film and then made a "B" line to the O'Club. I drank with the rest of the guys, discussed the mission, ate dinner with more talk and then start thinking about the next days mission again. I didn't know how many more of these I could take without really breaking down. I started to feel confused and paranoid.

# Chapter Eleven
# "Rest Time" (Combat Fatigue?)
## 27 May, '67 Mission #50
## Bac Giang Rd/RR Bridge, 25 Mi. NE Hanoi (NE RR)

I was not one to be superstitious, but following this mission in which my roommate, Capt Gordon "Buz" Blackwood was shot down, and the events preceding this mission, I became more and more that way. Maybe nothing to it, but in my mind, at the time, nothing was really making sense to me and I became one hell of a superstitious pilot. "Buz" was carried MIA for a long period of time, and in '73 when the POWs were returned, "Buz" wasn't one of them nor had any of the POW's remembered him being amongst them. In 1990, 23 years later, his remains were identified, and returned to the U.S. Officially, I remember seeing "Buz's" name crop up in Air Force Times as "declared KIA". This occurred before his remains were returned in '90, but the book on "Buz" closed at that point.

After this mission, I wondered about the events that preceded it. Whether it was a coincidence or not, we had several pilots shot down shortly after returning from an R&R where they met their wives or visited their families, or wore something new or different on a mission. These happenings were well known by many of the guys, and in fact, talked about, sometimes in jest (not that we thought there was anything funny about it) but we always tried to keep a sense of humor and not dwell on the unfortunate experiences of those who caught the golden B.B. We wanted to not believe that superstition had anything to do with anyone getting shot down. But in the back of your mind, the thought kept gnawing at you.

When I arrived at Takhli on Jan 30, 1967, new pilots were quartered in what was called a "hooch". I guess it was the Thai name for a barracks building, a single story, pre-fab, that contained metal cots and lockers for each pilot who stayed there. It held about 25 pilots. Each had a single cot and single locker. Belongings that didn't fit in the locker were usually stored in a foot locker which was placed in front of the cot or stored under the cot. The foot locker length was just long enough to fit the width of the cot but stuck out in the isle between the row of cots.

We were cramped to say the least. I was really surprised at these facilities since it reminded me of the old barracks we had when I went through pilot training in the early '50's at Hondo, Texas. Here, we were trying to fight a war with some very demanding hours and this didn't look like the way to get any rest.

The showers and lavatories were in a separate building, which was located adjacent to about four other hooches. We all shared the facilities. Wooden plank walkways led from each hooch to the shower/lavatory building.

That was my first home at Takhli when I arrived. I stayed there for about four weeks until a new facility that was under construction had been completed. This new BOQ was nicknamed the "Ponderosa". I don't know who

*"Hooch" living quarters at Takhli. (About 4 or 5 side by side) housed about 20 to 25 pilots each with side by side cots and foot lockers for storage of personal belongings. Thai maids washed clothes and hung them to dry outside on clothes lines outside hooches. Similar hooch buildings served as common shower and latrine areas for pilots living in these quarters.*

nicknamed it, but I suspect the name came from the TV series, "Ponderosa" which was popular during that time. These buildings were also single story, concrete, and housed 16 pilots, 2 to a room. They were quite comfortable, with a shower attached for each room of two, a toilet and wash basin. It afforded some privacy. This was a real improvement from the hooch living with 25 guys in an open bay affair, all having different flying schedules and sleeping hours. Some of us were up at 2:30 AM for mission briefings, while others tried to sleep in for the afternoon missions. It was difficult to get into a decent routine.

Pilots were offered "better" facilities, as rooms became available through attrition (others either finishing their 100 missions or shot down) based on arrival on station (seniority), and rank. In any event, I had the opportunity to move to the Ponderosa even though it was further from the squadron and wing flight line buildings. One pick up truck was assigned to each Bachelor Officer Quarters (BOQ) building for transportation. The use of it was determined by the pilots who lived in the BOQ. It took some scheduling and fixing of responsibility for the proper and efficient use of this one vehicle to satisfy the various schedules of each pilot. Not all pilots were in the same squadron and so we all had different schedules. Trying to find the guy with the vehicle keys was always a problem.

My first roommate at the Ponderosa was a young 1/Lt (Mathews) who happened to be my #4 wingman on the mission to Bac Le rail siding. A great young pilot who came out of the Training Command with very little fighter experience, but he did one hell of a good job. He flew wing during his entire 100 mission tour. That was hard to do, and still survive. He did!

When Lt. Mathews finished his 100 mission tour, "Buz" Blackwood, a young Capt, also from the Training Command, moved in as my roommate "Buz" was assigned to our squadron (333 TFS), but in a different flight than mine. He arrived at Takhli only about 2 or 3 days after me and had a few less missions than I at the time. He was doing well, and I was glad to have him as a roommate. "Buz" was easy to get along with, and we shared everything. We talked about our families, kids, Air Force career, such as it was. I always felt "Buz"

sort of looked up to me, only because I was older, a Major, and had a lot of fighter experience behind me. It was natural, but there was a lot of mutual respect.

"Buz" was married, had a son about 3 or 4 years old. He told me his parents were divorced but that he kept in contact with both parents. Around the end of April or first part of May, "Buz" received word that his father died. He decided to return to the states for the funeral.

Things were just starting to heat up in pack 6 about that time. The weather broke wide open in the Hanoi area around the middle of April. "Buz" left and was gone for about 2 weeks. Since he was in the

*Lenski in cockpit taken by "Buz."*

*Our (333 TFS) one pick-up truck for pilot transportation around the base, to and from Ops buildings and living quarters. Ed McCaffrey exiting truck.*

States, he decided to spend some time with his wife and son while he had the opportunity. Before "Buz" left, we asked one of the Weasel pilots in our BOQ to bring us back a Seiko wrist watch while he was in Okinawa on a R & R period. Having a Seiko watch was the in-thing to have, and one of the good deals at the time.

"Buz" returned around the third week in May, as I recall, and he was all fired up to get back into flying missions again and finish. The bombing missions to Hanoi area had increased while he was gone, and apparently he'd been following it in the papers back in the states and wanted to be filled in on all the details of what was going on.

Normally, on the day before the mission, we received the frag order for the next day. On the 26th, we knew our target for the 27th was the Bac Giang Rd/RR bridge, a JCS target. It was located on the northeast railroad, about 25 miles NE of Hanoi. Although "Buz" and I were in different flights in the same squadron, both of us were scheduled for the afternoon mission.

Following his return from the States, "Buz" flew a couple lower route pack sorties to get his proficiency and procedures back, but he had not been to pack 6 since his return. In fact, this was the first time to Bac Giang for both of us. Bac Giang Rd and RR bridge had not been hit for some time, so this was a target that needed to be taken out.

On my 35th mission, I'd been to Bac Ninh Rd/RR bridge, closer to Hanoi, just to the south of Bac Giang, about 15 miles from Hanoi. We had a lot of flak over the target that day and a lot of SAM activity but no Migs. But that was the 3rd of May and the Vietnamese had been rapidly building their defenses since then.

We knew one thing, the defenses, flak and SAMs would be greater and more accurate and the chances of Migs coming after us were also increasing. My 48th mission, only a week previous, on the May 20, was a good indication that the Migs would come at us. They lost 4 that day, so their tactics would probably change. One thing was for sure, they weren't going to give us a free ride.

The problem with these NE railroad targets were that during the last 2 or 3 minutes from the targets, we were in the flats which left us exposed without the hills to the north or south. Their radar could really track us well, and visually, we were always obvious as hell with all that black smoke trailing 20 F-105's and 4 F-4's as we came steaming in at about 500 feet, in afterburner, from the east.

It must have looked like a black cloud descending on them, and I'm sure that with all the noise associated with that armada of aircraft, it must have been one hell of a scary sight.

The night before the mission, "Buz" and I talked a lot and played some "Mama's and Papa's" records I bought at the Takhli PX. They were our favorites. We really liked their music.

"Buz" already knew about my experiences in pack 6 while he was gone and my hatred for the NE railroad targets. He was interested in the experiences I'd had so we discussed them, and I expressed my feelings and apprehensions about the white knuckler's to pack 6. We both knew the risk of being shot down was pretty high each time we went there. That was a "given" to everyone who had been to pack 6, and it only took one mission to realize it.

Our Seiko watches arrived the day before and they were great. Mine did not have a luminous dial or stop/reset feature for the second hand, which is used for time hacks, so I decided not to wear the Seiko for flying missions.

A time hack was given before each mission so we were expected to precisely meet the start engine, check-in, taxi, Take-off, tanker rendezvous, drop off, and Time Over Target (TOT) with precision accuracy. These times were especially important if you were a flight lead, and more important when you were the Strike Force or Deputy Force Commander. Even when I wasn't leading, I felt it to be a requirement for flying missions. I'd wait till I got back to the states and peacetime flying to wear the watch.

Besides, my G.I. watch, although not very nice looking, had all these features and it had been working well.

However, "Buz" decided to break in his new watch on the next day's mission!

We slept in and went to the O'Club for breakfast about 8:30 or 9 to catch the morning mission crews returning from pack 6 to see how they made out. We had breakfast, talked to the returning pilots and those who were going to be on the afternoon mission with us. We then made our way to the flight planning room in the Wing Hdq building for some target study time. We had plenty of time before briefing and lunch so we studied the target maps, cards and defense maps and some reccy photos of the target area. "Buz" came with me, and we both went through the routine of checking everything we could think of to be ahead of the force briefing.

"Buz" was flying with another flight in the 357 TFS even though he was in our squadron, the 333 TFS. This sometimes happened since the availability of pilots and the schedule for each of the three Squadrons didn't really fit the demand for the number of pilots available. His flight was scheduled as the last flight in the string of 5 F-105 flights in the force.

I was in the third flight, just in front of "Buz's" . Again, the tactic was for the four flights to bomb the target in a butterfly maneuver. That is, the first flight would bomb from one direction and the second from the other, 180 degrees out of sync etc. This seemed to work well in the past, so we continued to use this tactic, at least until I left in Aug '67.

We returned to the O'Club for lunch and again talked to the guys from the morning mission and I can only say that I envied them since they had already flown their mission that day and had returned safely, and I was just starting.

The briefing from the force commander was routine and the intelligence officer gave us the bad news on defenses in and around the Bac Giang area, reminding us that we were very close to Hanoi, Phuc Yen and Kep airfield. These were their major Mig airfields. We had already looked at the defense Maps for the area and saw the active flak and SAM site locations. There weren't many areas where you could not be in their range the last several minutes to the target and right over the target. The flak sites were all over the area. Every bit of the Northeast railroad was lined with both flak and SAM sites.

After the Force briefing at Wing Hdqs, we went to our respective Squadrons, for individual flight briefings. "Buz" went to the 357 TFS and later joined us at our 333rd TFS area. Usually we had about 45 minutes before engine start time, after our briefings. It was customary to conduct the individual flight briefings, and if time permitted play a couple games of bumper pool before we went to the aircraft. A bumper pool table was located in the small squadron lounge room in our squadron building. "Buz" and I always teamed up to play against the other squadron pilots whenever we had a chance. It helped take our mind's off the mission coming up. "Buz" and I had done pretty well at beating most of the guys in the Sqd and we looked forward to challenges from any two other guys. "Buz" and I played a couple games, did well as usual, but the time came to leave for the aircraft and the mission. Time was up!

We departed for the Personal Equipment (PE) room for our flight gear, got dressed in our G suits, survival vest, gun, left our rings and personal belongings on the shelf provided. We then got our survival radios checked by the PE guys, put our parachutes on, and proceeded to the ramp for our aircraft. It was routine!

"Buz" and I departed for the ramp together which was about 100 yds in front of the Sqd building. We crossed the familiar little walkway across a small wash which led to the ramp and the aircraft. The crickets and frogs were always making racket, day and night. As we crossed the small walk way, we wished each other luck, said we'd see each other when we got back and departed in different directions for our F-105's. That's the last time I saw Buz!

We refueled on Brown anchor off the Gulf, dropped off the tankers, F-4's joined up for Mig Cap and we were on our way to the IP at the lLe Madeleine, just off the east coast of pack 6, NVN.

We headed in with all the routine calls, Mig, SAM, and Radar guns. I don't remember any Migs being sighted on ingress or any SAMs being fired at us, however. We came to the end of the mountains (hills) and started into the flats about 2 or 3 minutes (at 9 mi/min) from the Bac Giang bridges. I could see the bridges over the river in the distance, very easy to pick up. Puffs of grey and black flak started to burst out in front of the first flight up front and then as the first flight got nearer the target, the whole sky exploded with white, grey, and black puffs as the force started to climb for the dive bomb run.

I was leading the third flight back and we would roll in from the North, in the opposite direction from the flight in front of us (butterfly attack). The flight in front started a left climbing turn and we followed in a right climbing turn about 30 seconds later, from the same point. The lead flight was in its bomb run and flak engulfed the entire flight. Their bombs were going off on the bridges and a lot of water being thrown up from the bombs as I concentrated on the target for my roll in point and dive bomb run.

As I climbed, flak was bursting all over us and a few black bursts with red fire balls were visible from those going off slightly in front and to either side. I had the flight echelon to the right for the roll-in, just before we started the pop maneuver. As I occasionally checked the flight to my right, I could see 2,3,&4 desperately hanging on in echelon. That gave me a good view of what the sky really looked like around us. Flak everywhere!

Anyway, I reached what I considered a good roll in point and initiated my roll in. I established a good dive angle, and as I focused on the target, I could pick up the red twinkling of the AAA guns from the flak sites as they fired at me. I say "me" because if you saw the guns fire (red out of the barrels), that meant the gun was pointed at you and you had about 4 or 5 seconds to move out of the line of fire or chances are, those bursts would nail you.

I got the pipper on the target as quick as I could, checked the airspeed and dive angle, made one pipper adjustment and pickled the bombs. (That took about about 4 or 5 seconds). I really didn't see the second flight from the south roll in because they had already come off the target and the last flight, ("Buz's") was just beginning their pop up from the south end of the target.

My flight joined up as we came off the target. I was relieved to see all of us join up without anyone being hit or knocked down. As a flight lead, you always felt good for an instant after the bomb run when you're joined up and untouched. The routine was to switch to discrete frequency after joining up from the bomb run to check each other over and talk without cluttering the strike frequency. We did, but continued to monitor Guard frequency. We egressed on discrete frequency until reaching the coast line and then switched back to strike frequency.

We rendezvoused with the tankers, and were getting refueled when the last flight approached and was also joining on their tanker. They were on a different tanker but on the same refueling frequency as my flight. My first clue that there was a problem was when their tanker boom operator asked the leader where their number 4 was or if they only had 3 F-105's for refueling. The lead came back with," Four won't be coming back, there are only 3 of us left".

This got my attention because I did not know which position in the flight "Buz" was flying. Furthermore, I didn't want to believe, at that point, that it was "Buz". My curiosity would have to wait till we got back to Takhli and debriefing.

After we landed, I quickly found out that It was "Buz" who had been shot down. I couldn't or didn't want to believe it. We were roommates, I had just talked to him a few hours before, as we left for the mission on the ramp. We played pool! We won! What the hell is this?. I thought, "This can't be!" I really cracked!

Apparently, "Buz" took a hit over the target from flak and no one in the flight saw it or a chute. He was # 4, the last F-105 in the force, tail end charlie. No beeper was heard either. He must have taken a really bad hit. Although no one actually knew what hit "Buz", it was probably AAA since there was very heavy flak over the target, and as the last aircraft in the force, every flak site in the area was probably shooting at him. After all, they had a lot of practice on the other 15 F-105's that preceded him.

After debriefing, I really didn't want to go back to the room. I spent the evening at the club trying to forget the whole mess. Going back to the room that night and looking at "Buz's" empty bed and belongings, as he left them, that morning, got to me.

The next day I decided to go to the Flight Surgeon for some sleeping pills to tide me over for the next couple days. I was really looking ragged. Since I was tired and probably looked it, he couldn't understand why I wanted sleeping pills. I explained to him how I felt about yesterday's mission and losing my roommate in addition to the letter I received from McCuistion's wife requesting more information on his shoot down back on May 8.

I asked his help to move me to another BOQ. I felt I needed to get away from there as soon as possible. The Surgeon listened to my problems without saying a word, as I recall, which I thought was strange at the time. Then he asked a few questions about how I felt, some personal feelings type questions, and after we finished, he told me that he was going to admit me to the hospital for some rest . He called it "battle fatigue" or "post something syndrome", and that all the experiences I'd had over the last several weeks were taking its toll and the best thing for me was a rest break. Not an R&R, but "sleep" type rest. He told me he would inform the Squadron Commander of my condition, not to worry about it and before I knew what was happening, I was admitted to the small dispensary hospital we had on base. I didn't fight it because it sounded like a good idea to me and I felt like I could sleep forever.

I slept for 24 hours. I actually felt like I lost a day. When I woke up, I remember not knowing exactly what day it was or how I got in the hospital. I had been completely bushed, worn out and tired. I ate like a horse and really was relaxing. I was feeling great again.

I was out in two or three days and I began to feel better about things. After all, I had a lot of time to think about what was happening. I thought, "What the hell, I had 50 missions now. I'm half way through with only 50 more to go! That was better than 51. Besides, things will change! This bad luck can't keep up like this. Things will get better!" At least I was thinking positive again.

# Chapter Twelve
# "Things Don't Get Better"
## Mission 51 Thru 60, 1-21 June, '67

Of the next nine missions, between 51 and 60, I'd been to pack 6, six times, the NE railroad (3), Thai Nguyen (2), and Phu Tho once. I had an R & R during this 4 week period. On June 17, I was scheduled to pack 6 for my 57th mission but never got further north than the Takhli traffic pattern.

I was recovering pretty well from the rest I'd had after my 50th mission and things were working out well. I was getting my confidence back and feeling good about going to pack 6 again. On June 17th, it wasn't pack 6 that almost got me, but an aircraft emergency on takeoff while breaking ground with a full load of bombs.

We were headed for Thai Nguyen on the afternoon mission and all the preparations had been accomplished with no unusual happenings. I had made a good preflight of the aircraft, checked the maintenance discrepancy form and talked to the crewchief about carried over discrepancies. Everything seemed in order.

Start up, and taxi out was normal. We were on our way "In Force" to pack 6. Our flight lined up on the runway for takeoff and I started my takeoff roll. I got the water injection, the afterburner (A/B) and things were looking good as I approached lift off speed. I rotated the aircraft and felt the aircraft lift off and then retracted the gear. All of a sudden I realized the stick was frozen when I tried to move it for minor corrections just after takeoff. A wing dropped and I naturally tried compensating for it, but the stick wouldn't move.

I thought I was imagining things at first, but then as I tried to move the stick fore and aft or lateral, I found it would not move. It was binding! Stuck! Frozen! The natural reaction is to use whatever you have to correct your flight path. I started to use my rudder for lateral control and pitch trim for pitch. It was working O.K. but I didn't know what was happening. Since I was just getting airborne after takeoff, loaded with 6/750 lb bombs and heavy as hell, I knew I was in trouble so I called the tower to declare an emergency. The rest of the flight was following me at about 10 secs apart and were airborne already so I told them to scramble the spare and that number three had the Lead because I was aborting with flight control problems.

One of my hydraulic pressure gages was slightly low but not low enough to cause the kind of problem I was having. It was more of a hard mechanical problem. Like a binding somewhere. The stick was frozen in fore and aft movements but occasionally I had some left and right lateral (aileron) movement. Very strange I thought. All I wanted was to get some altitude to jettison my bombs and punch out in case I really lost control of the aircraft.

I remained in burner long enough to get some altitude while I controlled the aircraft with the rudder and trim (when it worked). The Supervisor of Flying was offering advice from his position in Takhli tower. I needed to get rid of the bombs. I wasn't sure if I could control the aircraft enough to make it to the bomb jettison area several miles away and drop the bombs.

I finally agreed to make an attempt to jettison the bombs in the jettison area and then see if I could land the aircraft. I ruddered the crap out of the F-105 to baby it to the bomb jettison area and made one pass, safetied the bombs, and jettisoned them in the general area.

The control of the aircraft didn't improve, and I didn't expect it to. I still had two 450 gal fuel tanks full of fuel on board and needed to get rid of them or burn out the fuel. I jettisoned the fuel tanks also. Now all I had to do was get this thing on the ground or eject.

I decided to attempt a landing since I felt comfortable controlling the A/C up to this point. I hated the idea of ejecting, even in friendly territory.

I burned out most of the internal fuel circling around the area, and then put myself on a long final approach with a lot of time to see if I could control the aircraft during an approach to landing. All I had was rudder, throttle and airspeed to control the pitch and direction.

I set up a long final, adjusted the airspeed and landed using the rudder and throttle. On landing roll, I found the nose wheel steering working and used it to control the roll out. I could taxi fine. I was confused as hell about what was causing the problem. I taxied in behind the fire trucks and parked in the normal parking area, shut down and climbed out. The crew chief wanted to know what was the matter and I told him and wrote it up in the aircraft maintenance discrepancy form.

About a week later, I found out from maintenance that a pair of pliers was left in the aircraft's control stick well area during maintenance and that caused the stick to bind and lock up.

I was recommended for the 13th AF Well Done for this episode and it was later approved. A nice plaque, with pilot wings and an inscription of the episode. It hangs in my den today.

Shortly thereafter, another incident happened which was not associated with pack 6 but serious enough to cause me to think I was snake bit.

We had been executed on a pack 6 mission that afternoon and everything went normal as we taxied into the takeoff position with a flight of four. I was

*4/F-105Ds running up engines just prior to brake release for Take-off on Pack 6 mission. All loaded with 6/750 lb bombs.*

*F-105D about a 1,000 feet into take-off roll with afterburner and water injection cooking. Loaded with 6/750 lb bombs.*

flying Lead on this mission and lined up the flight as we normally did. We ran the engines up, element lead gave me the nod that he and four were ready and two indicated to me that he was ready also.

The weather was hot as usual and takeoff roll was computed and briefed during my briefing with the flight. The Engine Pressure Ratio, Eng Temp, etc all looked good during the run up, prior to releasing the brakes. One of the requirements we needed to pay attention to was getting "water injection" and an Afterburner (A/B) light as we released the brakes for takeoff. Sometimes you could get away with taking off on the available runway with no water injection but not without an A/B light. At least not with a full load of bombs on a hot day! All days were hot and muggy at Takhli.

A good rule to follow was, that if you did not get "water injection" or an A/B light, ABORT! One A/B re-light attempt was permissible, depending on the temperature and computed takeoff roll distance. In any event, I learned a very important lesson that afternoon about believing in the rules which have been tried and proven.

We were ready for takeoff, my head went back for the head nod that would start the timing for number two to start his clock for the 10 second separation between aircraft. I was at military power and everything checked out so I punched the water injection button and the green light came on and I could feel a slight increase in thrust, released the brakes and engaged the A/B at the same time. No afterburner Light! I already started to roll so I figured I'd try another light. So I came out of A/B with the throttle, waited a few seconds (normal to wait a couple seconds before attempting a re-light for the A/B nozzles and system to recycle) and then back into burner. No light again! I decided to try one more. I thought, surely it'll light this time. Within a few seconds, I realized how stupid this was.

I had just blown it. I was to far down the runway and to fast and heavy to stop on the remaining runway if I aborted with this full load of bombs and two 450 gal tanks full of fuel. Furthermore, even if the third attempt to light the burner was successful, their probably wasn't enough runway left to get off the ground. The problem was, I put myself in a coffin corner. I thought, "Dumb, Dumb, Dumb!

Now, I felt I had to continue and not abort. I had committed myself to continue the takeoff at any cost and take my chances. I came out of burner one more time, waited a few seconds and engaged the burner for the third attempt. She took! Even now, I didn't know if I had enough runway left to takeoff.

A lot of things were going through my mind at this point. I thought about jettisoning my fuel tanks but was afraid they would explode when they hit the runway, catch me up in the explosion and for sure the rest of the flight that was right behind me too.

Unknown to me at the time, the tower launched the fire trucks when they saw me accelerating slowly and continuing takeoff. I remember my number two in the flight calling me to see if I was O.K. since he had not seen my burner light-up. My response was always "Roger" even though things were not O.K.

I remember really being scared as I watched the end of the runway coming up fast and I didn't have enough speed to lift off. I waited till the very last part of the runway and last knot to rotate. I pulled back on the stick and the F-105 rotated quickly. I felt the end of the runway lip and roughness as the wheels bumped over the rough overrun before breaking ground. I raised the gear as soon as I could to reduce drag and tried to be as gentle as I could with the pitch attitude to just keep flying and not induce any drag.

I became airborne amid a cloud of dust from the burner which was blowing dust and crap from the end of the runway as I got airborne. The rest of the flight joined up and we were on our way to pack 6 with the rest of the Force for another counter toward the magic 100, grass, weeds and all.

# Chapter Thirteen
# "Direct Hit Over Thud Ridge"
## Mission 61, 22 June, '67 (Thai Nguyen Army Barracks)

I think this mission was the next closest I came to being shot down, except for the rescap mission on 30 April. Wolf Flight Lead, (Maj John Bobel) recorded this mission on a personal tape recorder carried aboard his aircraft. John's flight was the last flight in the force. We, Zebra flight were the 3rd flight in the strike force. His flight was just behind us in the string of the four bomb flights that struck the Thai Nguyen Army Barracks area on this mission.

During egress, after dropping our bombs on the target, I really took a bad hit that almost caused me to eject over Thud Ridge, in pack 6, where normally, no rescue attempt is made. The policy of no rescue in pack 6 was normal procedure. It was a lesson learned early in the war. Attempts were made, but <u>successful</u> attempts were very few. Too many rescue aircraft, particularly the helicopter rescue aircraft, were lost attempting to get downed pilots out when they were north of the Red River, in pack 6.

I always worried about being a victim of that policy, not that it wasn't a good policy, but because if I was ever hit in pack 6 and had to eject, I knew I was either going to be dead or a POW. Not a pleasant thought.

We were still going to pack 6 regularly in June since the weather continued to be good in the Hanoi area. We continued to be fragged into pack 6 on JCS targets, twice a day, every day, and the only thing that kept us from going was the weather. Since April, the weather had been excellent.

On June 22, the target was Thai Nguyen Army Barracks, just to the east of Thud Ridge. I'd been to Thai Nguyen several times already. The surrounding area was loaded with lucrative targets. The steel mill and railroad yard were those targets I'd already bombed, but this was the first time to the Army barracks.

Our call sign was "Zebra", a flight of four, and I was flying number two, on Maj Jim Baldwin's (lead) wing. Capt Dave Cobb was No. 3. All the mission preparations, takeoff, rendezvous with the tankers and the flight to the Red river were normal. We had the usual SAM and Mig warnings as we approached the Red River, and we knew they had picked the force up early and were getting their defenses ready. We crossed the Red at the same old turn point, headed for the river "Y" which was another turn point at the northwest end of Thud Ridge.

We plugged in the burner as we crossed the Red River turn point and were accelerating as usual, keeping our spacing on the flight in front. We pressed on a few more miles to the river "Y" and Thud Ridge where we turned southeast along the south side of the ridge. A few more miles along the ridge was our final I.P which was the 5223 foot peak, the highest point on the ridge. From this I.P., it was only about one and a half minutes to the target at the speed we were traveling (9 mi/min). From there, the Army Barracks was not hard to find.

The Force pressed on to the target, without problems other than the normal SAM warnings, flak starting to appear over the target area, and a few SAM firings which did not disrupt the force. The lead flight was already in their bomb run as we started our pop up maneuver for the roll in with 37, 57, and 85 millimeter AAA going off all over us, as usual. Since we were the third bomb flight to strike the target, a lot of dust, smoke, and debris obscured the target. We finally rolled in, dropped our bombs on the target and came off successfully without anyone taking a hit. Now we began the all important maneuvering to rejoin as a flight. Once we came off the target, it was routine, but a challenge to locate the leader for join up. The last thing you wanted to do was come out by yourself (a straggler). If that happened, you were a prime Mig and SAM target, waiting to be tapped. Our flight (Zebra) was headed back out to the Ridge the same way we came in, trying to rejoin for egress.

As We came off the target, I had Jim Baldwin (Zebra 1) insight. He was making a left turn to the west for the Ridge and the peak. I was accelerating to catch him as quick as I could, and as I started to close on him from his right side, he started a right turn to parallel the ridge. I started to cut him off in the right turn and realized I had a lot of overtake speed on him.

I was closing fast and knew I'd overshoot him, so I came out of burner and started a climb to kill some airspeed. This would put me above Lead and slightly above the Ridge which was immediately in front of us. I pulled up in a right banking turn, pulling some G's as I turned right, sliding high on Jim's left wing, against the ridge.

As I reached the peak of my climb, with about 60 degrees of bank, against the side of the ridge, pulling hard with a lot of G's, and starting to synchronize my speed for a join up, I heard this tremendous explosion, "BANG". A hell of a jolt! I immediately knew I'd taken a hit. The cockpit filled with smoke. Debris was flying all over me in the cockpit.

I had white smoke and vapor, or whatever it was, along with dust and crap from the cockpit flying around me, along with the smell of something burning. It was all simultaneous. I was dazed at first!

I transmitted that I was hit. At first, I didn't give a call sign, so I transmitted it again with my call sign.

The audio tape indicates I said, "I' m hit,..... Zebra two, I'm hit!"

I have finally realized after being hit a few times that this sort of communication comes instinctively. Your first reaction is to speak, say something to someone.

I told Jim (Zebra Lead) I'd been hit and had smoke in the cockpit. He immediately slowed down and joined on me and told me to take the lead. Jim had me in sight off to his left wing since I had almost completed a join-up on him.

The gear horn was blasting in my ear, and red and yellow warning lights were staring me in the face. Junk and stuff were still flying around in the cockpit.

I punched the gear warning horn silence button and the Master Warning and Caution lights off too. I looked at my gages to see what the problems were. My airspeed and altimeter tapes were inoperative. The Horizontal Situation Indicator (HSI) or directional gyro was also out, frozen. Hydraulic gages looked good, and then I came to the Oil Pressure gage. It read zero ("0")!

I felt a big lump in my throat and my heart sunk! I thought, "That's It"! I'm screwed! The engine will only last for another couple minutes, that is, if I'm lucky! I called Jim again and told him I didn't have any oil pressure on the gage and relayed the rest of the problems as I saw it in the cockpit.

I knew that the engine does not sustain any more stress on the main bearing in afterburner as it does in military power, so I had nothing to lose by using the afterburner to get as much thrust as I could out of the engine before it froze for lack of oil.

One thing I didn't want to do was jockey the power or reduce thrust with no oil pressure. (This happened to me in an F-86 when I was a young Lt. in '59, and that baby froze up within seconds after I reduced power). I told Jim I was engaging the burner to get as fast and as high as I could so that if the engine froze, and I had to bail out, I'd have a chance of getting across the Red River for rescue.

At that point, I was convinced that I was going to have to eject in a few minutes. I wanted to get across the Red River first so that some sort of rescue effort could at least be made.

The majority of my instruments were out and I didn't know how fast I was going, the direction, nor my altitude. Since it was a clear day, I was VFR and could navigate out of the area without a problem.

Lead (Jim Baldwin), followed me and gave me directions. I immediately made a left turn to the southwest to get across the Red as quick as I could. I asked Jim if I should jettison the "Multiple Ejection Rack" (MER) which hangs under the belly of the aircraft to carry the bombs. He responded that it was already gone. I thought, "I didn't jettison it, so I must have taken the hit under the belly and that's what caused the MER to come off."

Two gages I didn't pay attention to, on retrospect, that got me in trouble later were the Oxygen gage and the cockpit pressurization Altimeter.

As I started to climb, Jim reminded me of the Yen Bai SAM site just ahead and I was headed right for it. He suggested that I remain at low altitude instead of climbing to avoid being picked up by the SAM site. Good thinking!

I thought about that for a few seconds and was torn between staying low with the engine getting ready to quit or climb and being subjected to the SAMs from Yen Bai. I decided to stay at low altitude as Jim suggested. Jim hung in there with me the whole way keeping me advised of the SAM threat. Jim was as vulnerable as I, but he stayed with me the whole time.

I figured I had about a minute until the engine froze without oil. I was almost at the Red and that's really all I hoped for. I could always climb and glide a few miles after it quit at the speed I was traveling.

Still in burner and going almost supersonic, Jim called and said I was smoking, and that I'd better slow it down and come out of burner. I thought, "this is it!" I paused, came straight out of burner without reducing the throttle and waited for it to freeze. It didn't!.

I crossed the Red and she was still running. What a break! I began thinking about ejection at this point and started to stow maps and all loose equipment. These were things I had positioned up on both sides of the Windscreen which I wanted handy during the mission. I took my knee pad off and stowed it behind me, on the right side, in the map case.

Then I started to think about what the procedures were for rescue after I got on the ground. I drew a blank! I started to panic! I couldn't remember anything about what I was suppose to do first.

I almost punched the mike button to ask Jim what I was suppose to do after I ejected and got on the ground. Do I hide my chute? Shoot flares? I was really panicking and confused. I tried to recall what the survival instructors had said about survival procedures after hitting the ground and couldn't remember anything. I was afraid to call Jim and ask such a stupid question.

While I'm doing all this thinking, I'm listening to Red Dog Lead (Col Bill Norris, the Force Commander and my Squadron C.O.) try to contact Crown to set up a rescue effort. He told them to move the tankers north and get the rescue Sandies and Helicopters moving north for a possible rescue effort. Col Norris was doing things right and I was happy to hear he was taking charge.

I hoped that it wouldn't turn out like the Carbine 3 rescue effort on April 30.

About 3 or 4 minutes had passed and the engine was still running so I began to wonder that maybe the oil gage might be out like my other tape and gyro instruments. I hoped that was true. I had no way of telling. The circuit breakers were all in and electrical power was good. I was waiting for the next "gottcha."

I left the power alone and kept pressing south with Jim on my right wing. He was giving me altitudes, airspeed and headings like a Ground Control Approach (GCA). We were VFR so it wasn't that difficult. After about 7 or 8 minutes, we decided the oil gage was probably inoperative or the engine would have quit by now. I was relieved and started to feel like I may not have to jump out of this thing after all.

At one point, I asked Jim how far we were from Ch 97 which was just across the North Vietnamese border to the south, in Laos. He said about 45 miles. He then added that he thought I could start climbing. I started to climb for as much altitude as I could get. We climbed to about 37,000 ft by the time we hit Ch 97 and when I asked what my airspeed was, Jim said, 360 Kts indicated.

We asked Crown to have the radar control facility (call sign "Brigham") come up on our frequency. They did and we got vectors to Udorn for recovery. They told us that the Sandies had been launched out of Udorn and on their way to meet us if we needed them. Things were sounding like they were falling in place for a rescue effort if I needed it.

The frequencies were filled with transmissions over Guard, and our main frequency. Crown was transmitting on the rescue frequency and Mig warnings were still being transmitted on Guard. All these transmissions filled the air, with some transmissions being blocked out. This was typical, however.

We didn't want to attempt a refueling since we thought we had enough fuel to get to Udorn. We didn't want to delay getting on the ground.

After we leveled off at altitude, somewhere between the NVN border and Udorn, I began to feel uncomfortable. My stomach was starting to act up and I was beginning to feel funny. Finally, I realized I might be hypoxic. I looked at the oxygen supply gage, and it was at zero. I looked at the standby altimeter and it read 37,000 ft. I knew then what was happening. I'd lost pressurization as a result of the hit and whatever took out my other gages and instruments must have depleted my oxygen supply too.

I was really feeling lousy. I called Jim and told him I thought I was getting hypoxia, no oxygen, or pressurization. I had already started to descend and he said I'd better take it down as quick as I could. I made a high speed descent and got down to about 14,000 ft and immediately started to feel better. I continued down to 10,000 ft and leveled there for the rest of the flight back to Udorn.

As we got closer to Udorn, we contacted the tower and told them our problem and requested landing instructions.

I remember that after I was hit, the landing gear warning horn was blowing. I told Jim that I might have a gear problem and I wanted to lower the gear and have him check it over while we were still a ways out. He agreed, so I slowed down and tried to put the gear handle down, but the gear handle in the cockpit was stuck in the up position. It wouldn't move!

Although I suspected some sort of gear problem, getting the gear handle down was not one of them. I banged on it, even tried to kick it down with my left foot but it would not budge. I couldn't get my leg in a good position even after I unstrapped my seat belt and shoulder harness. The stick was in the way and I couldn't maintain control of the aircraft very well while trying to kick the gear handle. I used all the force I could muster, but couldn't move it. I thought, "What a mess, what else is wrong with this airplane"?

Things just kept getting worse each time I tried to check a system. Now I was faced with a gear up landing. I was losing my sense of humor, if there was any humor in this whole mess.

I briefed Jim on my problem and he gave me some procedures which might help move the handle, but none worked. We checked everything we could think of. We were approaching Udorn and getting low on fuel which might be O.K. if you're going to land gear up and want to avoid a large fuel fire caused by the sparks on a belly landing. I preferred to continue to try and get the gear handle down somehow. For all I knew, even if I got the gear handle down, I wasn't sure the gear would come down and locked. That may be another problem, who knows?

I called the tower and appraised them of my gear problem and requested fire trucks standing by and asked if they could foam the runway? They said they could foam the runway, but it would take about 15 minutes. I said foam half the width of the runway for about the first two thirds. They did, while I circled overhead and continued trying to get the gear handle down without success.

Jim stayed with me, trying to help. He intended to go back to Takhli without having to refuel but with the delay, he called for a tanker for refueling in case he needed it after he finished chasing me.

The runway was finally prepared. Crash trucks were standing by, and I proceeded to a high key point for a precautionary gear up landing. I started to feel the pressure of the thought of landing this way and a possible fire on the landing. It worried me.

I had no choice! I had to get this bird on the ground before something else happened or I ran out of fuel. I hit high key and started a wide turn for base and final. Jim kept calling off airspeed and altitude to me as I continued to beat on the gear handle, trying to get it down. I still had not given up!

Somewhere on a downwind leg, one of the hard bangs I gave the gear handle, sent it to the down position. I could feel the gear come out almost simultaneously, but I had no gear lights at all. Jim called to tell me the gear was coming down. I asked him to give me a visual check since I didn't have any gear lights. He slid underneath me to look at the gear and told me the gear looked down and locked. I couldn't believe it.

I had no choice at that point to do anything else but land on this approach even if the gear didn't look locked. I was running out of gas. I was still not sure about the oil problem or any other systems on the airplane so I pressed on and hoped for the best. it was comforting to know that the gear looked down and locked.

I told the tower I had a visual gear down and locked condition with no lights to indicate safe or unsafe. The gear warning horn was not on so I felt that maybe the gear was locked since the horn did come on after I took my hit and stayed on until I turned it off. I thought it was still functional and if I had an unsafe condition, it would probably be on now. I decided to land on the side of the runway without the foam and take my chances of a safe gear.

Coming down final seemed like a long time. Jim was still keeping me advised of airspeed and altitude on final approach.

A lot of thoughts went through my mind in this short period of time. Not just about what might happen if the gear collapses, but about this whole damn tour. I thought, "Even if I make this O.K., I still had about 39 more missions left, and when will my luck run out?" I even thought of Bettye and the kids, and wondered where they were at this time.

I started to round out over the overrun, held the aircraft off in a nose high attitude so I could make an easy touch down in case the gear didn't hold. Jim kept calling off airspeeds to me until he couldn't stay with me anymore as I slowed up in the round out for landing. The landing felt smooth, and I fought to keep it straight as I eased the nose down slowly until the nose wheel touched down and held. Then I knew I had it made! I felt great. As I deployed the drogue chute, I could hear Jim's F-105 above me as he passed me about 50 feet. He lit the burner and started a steep climb heading south to a tanker and Takhli. What a beautiful sight.

I called and transmitted my thanks to Jim for all the assistance as he flew out of sight. I stopped with plenty of runway left except there was a lot of foam on the runway which I hadn't used that needed to be cleaned up.

I taxied off the runway, shut it down and let the tow truck pull me in to wherever they wanted me. I remember doing this about 6 weeks ago on my 34th mission.

I couldn't wait to park and find out what the damage was to the aircraft. They parked me and took their time looking the aircraft over before they put a ladder up to the cockpit so I could climb out. The crew chief had found the hit and the damage in the nose wheel well when he put the nose gear pin in. That's where most of the major damage occurred.

The hole was in the left front side of the nose of the aircraft, just above and to the right of the M-61 Vulcan 20-MM cannon barrel. It was a fairly clean rip about 2 to 4 inches only. It had penetrated into the nose wheel well where the oxygen tank is located. It severed a lot of wires in the wheel well which pro-

*Photos of the damaged Horizontal Situation Display Instrument (HSDI or HSI) from my instrument panel of the F-105 flown on my 61st mission to Thai-Nguyen, 22 June '67.*

vides power to the instruments in the cockpit and punctured the oxygen tank.

This was an armor piercing round that cleanly penetrated everything, including the instrument panel and the rear of the Horizontal Situation Display (HSI) instrument (about an eighth inch thick) which was located right in front of me in the cockpit. The hole in the rear of the HSI was round and melted around the edges, but a nice clean, round hole. The round penetrated the HSI about 4 inches destroying a bunch of wires before it finally came to rest.

I have that HSI as a souvenir. It sits in my home next to all the other North Vietnam memorabilia I kept from this tour.

Although it didn't look like much from the outside of the aircraft, all the wires it cut in the nose wheel well, and damage it did as it penetrated the oxygen tank and instrument panel really raised hell with all the systems. At least I understood why I had the gear horn on, all the warnings and instrument indications, real and false, in the cockpit.

I was lucky as hell that the round did not penetrate any further, because the HSI sits right in front of the pilot and the stick. I had lucked out again and wondered how much longer it would last.

I remember the crewchiefs and Intelligence officers, who debriefed me, asking if I was the one who had been there several weeks ago with the other F-105 that was damaged. They remembered me from the last time I landed with battle damage, and so did I. I had to wait a while to be debriefed by Intelligence because they were debriefing a Recce pilot (RF-101) after being shot down the day before. He had just been picked up and returned to Udorn. His name was Capt Bob Patterson. I'll never forget it! When he came out of debriefing, he looked good, a few lacerations on his face from the parachute risers but I think he looked better than me. We talked for a long time about our missions and each could relate to the other's anxiety and frustrations of combat and with the war as it was being fought. I found out from the conversation we had that the Recce pilots were just as frustrated as we were. I hoped that was the last time I would have to spend the night at Udorn. I was beginning to feel at home there.

# Chapter Fourteen
## Missions 62 to "Golden" 95

After being hit on Thud Ridge, until I reached my 95th mission, things started to settle down. I had missions that I felt like nothing would happen and those that I did not feel comfortable with at all. The tour was becoming more psychological than anything else. I had conjured up a lot of unpleasant scenarios that would happen on each pack 6 mission and was convinced it would take place.

A lot of the guys in the squadron knew I was having a rough time of it so one of the guys conned a Thai waitresses at the O'Club to pin a Buddha pin on my flight suit during lunch before one of my pack 6 missions. It was supposed to bring good luck, and supposedly, nothing bad would happen to me.

I was sitting at the table eating lunch when this young Thai waitress came up to me and said something in broken English about a good luck charm. I was taken by surprise, and stopped eating. I tried to listen to what she was saying. The guys at the table were laughing and of course they knew what it was all about. I couldn't understand what she was saying, and then one of the guys explained the meaning of the Buddha pin and that she was only trying to give me a pin which would protect me during the rest of my missions. I really was taken aback.

She pinned it on my flying suit, and I wore it the rest of my tour, on every mission.

Superstitious? I guess!

It's ironic that of the 33 missions left to reach 95, I flew about 22 to pack 6 and had less problems than the first 11.

## Stuck Throttle

On one of my missions to the NE Railroad, which took us over the gulf for ingress and egress, I had a problem which was not related to battle damage but nonetheless caused a problem which could have resulted in an ejection over the north.

We had hit our target at the NE railroad in pack 6, and had egressed successfully. We rendezvoused with the post strike tankers and were refueling over the gulf. I was on the tanker and had almost taken on all of the fuel I needed for recovery to Takhli, but as I jockeyed the power to stay in a refueling position for the last bit of fuel, the throttle froze. I could not move it back or forth. The throttle setting was at about 98% power. I was still on the refueling boom and taking on fuel but couldn't back off or accelerate. I called for an emergency disconnect and left the tanker with fuel streaming off the boom, and as usual, residual fuel fumes entered the cockpit. I couldn't control the power. I slid under the tanker and came up on the right side, and tried to control my airspeed by climbing and descending.

I had enough fuel on board with the fuel flow at the stuck power setting to make it to Takhli, so I didn't need to refuel again. The rest of the flight refueled, and we departed for Takhli, west, across route pack 1 in North Vietnam.

I thought about by situation, and decided to try to free the throttle. I tried to pull the throttle back with all the force I could muster, over and over again, as we started on our westerly heading back to Takhli. We were still over the gulf and just starting to cross the coast line into North Vietnam. I was still trying to free the throttle by pulling it back, but it would not move. I was getting impatient and mad as hell, yanking as hard as I could to free it. Suddenly, I realized where I was. Over North Vietnam! Dumb! I thought, "If I succeed in pulling the throttle back by freeing it, it may not go back forward again. I may even stop-cock it and either way, I may have to eject—over North Vietnam." I thought, "How dumb! Leave things alone until you get to Takhli and then try to free the throttle." All this time, I was yanking back and pulling back on the throttle to reduce thrust. Really dumb!

As we approached Takhli, and entered within radio contact of the tower, I advised them that I had a stuck throttle and would have to make an emergency landing. Furthermore, I told them to recover the rest of the returning force of F-105s first, since I may end up closing the runway in my attempt to land.

They agreed and got every one on the ground as I held overhead, burning off fuel, reading the emergency check list for "Landing with a stuck Throttle."

All the aircraft recovered, and now it was my turn. The tower had the fire trucks standing by along the runway for any eventuality. The barrier at the far end of the runway was up and so was the cable. I felt better about that!

The Supervisor of Flying (SOF) had read the check list procedures to me and felt that we had the plan down pat. I'd make my approach with a long final approach and reduce airspeed by zig zagging on final with the gear down to keep the airspeed from increasing. I felt comfortable with being able to do that.

I had already experimented with controlling the aircraft in that manner and it was not to difficult to do. The problem I saw, was stopping the engine (running at 98%) after I landed. I'd have to shut the fuel switches off just prior to landing and hope that the engine would quit within the time frame the Tech order advertised (10 secs). If the engine didn't quit within that time frame, the procedure suggested the use of the afterburner to purge the residual fuel to flame the engine out. I thought that made sense unless there was enough fuel in the lines to actually provide for an afterburner light and thrust I didn't want, and at the wrong time.

I maneuvered on to a long final to the north (landing to the south), slowed the aircraft down by speed brakes and pulling G's in a steep bank, reversing my turn, and yanking and banking. I lowered the gear and flaps and set up a low, long final approach, turning occasionally to keep the speed down. Time was getting short, and I wondered how this dumb thing would end. I thought, "after all these missions and all I've been through to survive, wouldn't this be a stupid way for it to end".

As I passed over the approach lights, and what I considered to be about 10 secs from touchdown, and with enough airspeed to make a landing, even if the engine quit immediately, I turned the master fuel switches off. I believe there were about 4 pump switches and the master switch. I had my left hand

and fingers on the switches all the way down final so I would not have to fumble at the last couple of seconds.

With the fuel switches off, the engine kept running at 98% (almost full power). I rounded out and was having to force the aircraft on the ground with the engine still cooking. I thought, "When will this thing quit?" I was on the ground and on a landing roll, but going like hell. I deployed the drogue chute. It slowed me down only momentarily until the chute was blown off by the jet blast.

I lowered the tail hook in preparation for a barrier engagement. The end of the runway was coming up fast. I was getting ready to go outboard with the throttle to engage the afterburner, as suggested in the tech-order, when the engine quit very suddenly. I was on the brakes but then realized, all the systems will shut down with the engine driven pumps shut down, so I pulled the emergency brake handle (compressed air instead of hydraulic fluid for brakes with only about 3 pedal applications) and got on the brakes with one fairly hard application. The brakes held and as I approached the cable, the nose wheel went over it slowly and I stopped before I engaged the barrier with the tailhook which hung down from the bottom rear end of the F-105. I was dead in the water but safe with no damage to the aircraft.

I was towed back to the parking area, debriefed, and then started to think about the next day's mission. I was tired and hungry. A good sign!

I later found out that the hardened steel, "spring like", dust cover (about 2 inches wide and the length of the throttle quadrant) that followed the throttle fore and aft had broken and jammed the throttle. There was no way to move it except by taking the whole quadrant apart and replacing the metal dust cover spring, which they did.

## The Golden Rule Changes

Since the tail end of June, all of July, and into the 1st week of August, I'd been hitting pack 6 hot and heavy, and I was really getting punchy. I had reached my 86th mission on July 25th, and I thought, "I only had 4 more to turn golden, (90) and then I would only have 10 more in the lower route packs." I was looking forward to that as sort of a reprieve.

I always hated the NE railroad, and in particular the Kep railroad yard target. I thought I was getting only one more crack at it on my 87th (31 Jul). But that was followed by Thai Nguyen (88); a RR tunnel, NE of Thai Nguyen (89); and a RR siding south of Thai Nguyen (90) which at the time, should have been my last pack 6 mission. I remember thinking about really putting out on this last pack 6 mission and being careful but effective. One last parting shot at Ho Chi Minh's back yard, number 90.

So after attacking the target and dropping the bombs, I remember feeling great, and on egress, after crossing the red river heading south, I looked back to take one more look at the Hanoi area and pack 6. I wanted to look at the place that had humbled me so greatly! I'd met the magic number of missions, 90 up north, and now the last 10 would be to the lower NVN route packs where I felt it would be a piece of cake to finish up with easier missions. Little did I know that I'd be back to pack 6 two more times after my 90th and before I finished 100.

After landing, I debriefed the mission with Intelligence, then proceeded to the photo Intelligence area to look at my bomb film. I was feeling good knowing I only had 10 more missions to complete the tour, then home!

After debriefing, I proceeded to the operations and mission planning area where the large mission scheduling board was located. The large scheduling board would have the missions, pilots, aircraft, bomb loads etc. for the next days missions. I wanted to see who was on the missions and what lower route pack missions might be scheduled.

One of the Intelligence officers came into the room and was making changes to the scheduling board. I asked him what the changes were and he told me, but also added that the Wing had changed the golden rule from 90 to 95 missions because of lack of qualified pack 6 pilots.

I couldn't believe what he said and thought, "this can't be true. I just completed 90 and now they decide to change the rule. Just my luck!" It was true, and my name was on the schedule for the JCS target, Kep rail yard on the NE railroad, for tomorrows mission.

Now I was really paranoid! At this point, I really thought someone or something was out to get me. I'd finished my 90 missions like everyone else that preceded me, I hated Kep and the northeast railroad where we lost so many guys, and now, the day I reach 90, they change the rules. Not only that, but I was now scheduled to Kep railyard, the worst target in the system. I thought, "was the world against me, or what?"

I knew in my own mind that this was it! My last mission. I wouldn't come back.

I went to the O'Club and had a few drinks with the rest of the guys and laughed and scratched as we joked about the new policy. I figured I was a dead man. I really believed it!

As it turned out, I survived Kep one more time, on Aug 5, '67, and made it back, much to my surprise.

## The Last Pack Six Mission

The next three missions were in the lower route packs but then for my 95th mission, I was back in the barrel one more time.

On 9 Aug ,'67, we were scheduled to the Vinh Yen RR Yard (NW of Phuc Yen airfield). Phuc Yen airfield was off limits to us at that time, and they had a lot of guns on the field to fire at anything within a 5 mile or so radius. It was the largest airfield in North Vietnam with Mig 21s and 17s. We were prohibited from striking it by our own rules but yet, they launched Migs and fired their AAA guns at us daily, and we were restricted—by our own government—from attacking this most lucrative target.

In any event, this target didn't seem like a piece of cake because of its proximity to Phuc Yen airfield. I felt it was an easier target than the NE railroad though. I still had that nagging feeling about being shot down and that this was it, again. I felt that even if I got back from this one, they will change the rules again and I'll end up going back to pack 6 till I reach 100 anyway.

I had lost all confidence in the system and any rules about going to pack 6. I began to prepare myself for flying to pack 6 to the bitter end and maybe more.  The funny part about it was that I was beginning to laugh about it and really began to not care anymore.

We ingressed to the target via the normal ingress route we'd always taken. We Hit the Red River I.P., at the loop in the river where we turned toward the river "Y" I.P. near Thud Ridge, then southeast down the Ridge.  This time we broke off at the end of the ridge, just short of Phuc Yen airfield, where the road and the railroad met, SE of of a small village.

The guns at Phuc Yen airfield were putting up a layer of flak you could walk on.  AAA puffs were opening up all over the place as though they were expecting us.  No SAM's or Mig's attacked us, just AAA.

We dropped our bombs on the RR yard and headed out toward the ridge and no one was hit.  Egress was uneventful despite the flak.  As we proceeded up the ridge, it dawned on me one more time that this was hopefully the last time I'd see pack 6 and the ridge.

To some extend, it was like realizing you wouldn't be back to something that meant a lot to you.  I can't explain it, but although I was so happy to know this was my last pack 6 mission, at the same time, there was some sorrow associated with it.  I'd seen so many of our guys shot down here, but the ridge protected me.  It was as though we were friends, and I was leaving.  A very funny feeling indeed.

As we turned south from the end of the ridge and crossed the Red River, I had to look back at the Hanoi area and pack 6 one more time to once and for all fix that picture in my mind, because I knew I would never want to forget it. I had learned so much about war, feelings, and myself, that this picture, in my mind, would always remind me of these things which could never be experienced anywhere else, and I did not want to forget.

To this day I have that picture framed in my mind.  I still feel like I know the ingress and egress routes, and targets I'd bombed.  I know I won't forget the memories that still exist in my mind of pack 6.

## Planning The Doumer Bridge Raid

After I arrived back from this, my 95th mission, I fully expected that I would be required to continue going to pack 6 until I completed 100 missions. I also hoped I was wrong.

As usual, I was wrong! 95 was it! My last 5 could be in the lower route packs. I was overjoyed.  I immediately went to the flight planning room after my debriefing and found out that we had just received the fragmentation order to strike the JCS target we'd been sitting on for the past week, the "Doumer Bridge". I had mixed emotions now, about not being able to participate on this mission.

While I was there in the briefing room, the intelligence folks came out to change the target to the Doumer Bridge.  Our new Vice Commander, Col Bob White (Astronaut) walked in right behind them and erased the Strike Force Commander's name on the scheduling board and inserted his name.

I was surprised, since he had not been with us very long and did not have a lot of missions under his belt.  I was impressed by his courage and eagerness, but wondered if he knew what he was getting into.  In any event, later that evening, my Squadron Commander, Lt/Col Bill Norris and I were asked to help Col White plan the mission to the Doumer Bridge since we were senior guys with experience, getting ready to finish our 100.

By the time I arrived at the flight planning room, as I recall, plans were being made to ingress directly to the Bridge from the south which would take the force across the city of Hanoi on ingress. This was a completely different route than we normally used. Bearing in mind that the Doumer Bridge had not been targeted for at least 6 months because the area around Hanoi (10 mile circle) had been off limits for that length of time. This ingress approach being planned would be a dead give away to a Hanoi target-the Doumer Bridge.

My advice was to go in the same way we always had. Ingressing, across the Red at the same turn point, southeast down the ridge to the end, and from there, a short distance south, down the north railroad and to the Doumer Bridge. We had used this same route to strike the the North railroad just outside the 10 mile ring, the Thermal Power Plant, north of Hanoi and the railroad just outside the circle. It was only about 30 more seconds to the Doumer Bridge from other targets in the general area that we had hit and this, I argued, would give an element of surprise. The egress would be different than other missions, however. Egress should be to the south, I argued. That is, hit the target and keep going south across the Red which would be the shortest route to get into a rescue area for anyone that might be hit and have to eject.

It made sense in this case, not to change the ingress routing. I felt that was the key!

The egress was being planned to go back up Thud Ridge after striking the target from the south, which would expose the force to a longer period of time in pack 6 to SAM's, Migs and everything else they threw at us on the way out. The probability that someone would take a hit and have to eject was very high. Therefore, it also made sense to have a quick egress for a good chance of any rescue effort that might be needed.

The rescue effort was always in the back of my mind. Many of the pilots that were still trying to complete there missions had not had the experience of participating in rescue efforts behind them. I did, twice, and both times they were gut wrenching failures, so I was very sensitive about planning for the best way in and out in case someone got shot down. I wasn't sure everyone realized the importance of that kind of planning before the mission.

In any event, after much discussion, the mission was planned to ingress and egress as Bill Norris and I suggested. Bob White and the rest of the planning group agreed that that was the better option. I didn't participate in that mission, but the next day when it took place (Aug 11), I followed every minute of it from briefing to debriefing. It was like going on the mission with the force. I agonized the entire time they were gone, wondering what was happening. When they returned, everyone made it back. No one was shot down, but a couple had taken some damage. The mission was a successful one to the point of actually dropping a span of the Doumer Bridge. What made me feel good was that all the guys came back O.K. and no one had gone down. That meant a lot to me!

I felt that I had contributed to the mission success even though I had not flown it. My concern now was to complete 100 missions. For me, only five more missions were left to fly.

# Chapter Fifteen
# *Finally "100"*
## *(18 Aug, 1967)*

When our Wing Commander, Col Bob Scott completed his tour, Col (MGen., Ret) John C. Giraudo took command of the 355th TFW. His reputation was well known and impressive. For the short period of time that I knew him, he lived up to it and then some. One hell of a guy! Since I was one of the few in the "golden" category, I was assigned to check him out in the lower route packs before he went to pack 6. I felt honored to be checking out someone with his past combat record and experience which included WWII combat and (POW), Korea combat and (POW), and now fighting in Vietnam. I thought, Jesus, all I need to do is have him shot down again, with me as the leader, and that will really cork it. I wondered if he had been told how snake bit I had been.

Ninety-six thru ninety-nine were uneventful in the lower route packs. The missions were few and far between since the concentration with available aircraft in the wing to support the strike force to pack 6 twice a day (20 A/C plus 2 spares, each mission) taxed the maintenance capability.

My 100th mission occurred on August 18. It was scheduled as a flight of four to route pack 1 to work with a forward air controller (FAC) "Misty" call sign, near Mu Gia Pass. Misty's were also referred to as "Fast Fac's", an F-100 aircraft. They were known for finding very lucrative targets to hit, as apposed to an O-1, A-1 or OV-10 FAC type aircraft.

Our new Wing Commander, Col Giraudo, was scheduled with me, and I believe he flew as number 3, with me as lead. We were to rendezvous with the FAC in route pack 1, drop our ordnance (6X750 lb bombs each) on whatever target they may have for us. We briefed the mission, safe areas, in case someone was shot down, all the defenses in the area and rescue procedures. It seemed like a routine mission.

It was also a tradition for the pilots completing their tour that on their 100th mission they would be allowed to make a flyby after return to base. So I briefed the flight what I intended to do as a 100 mission type celebration which wasn't a whole hell of a lot. I was not going to get carried away with any fancy air show over the base. We had a few incidents occur as a result of over indulgence in some of the 100 mission fly overs. I was content to make a high speed pass with maximum performance climb over the field and then land without any fancy maneuvers. I just wanted to finish the assigned mission first, and for sure, not have an incident during some sort of self indulging air show that could end up in a disaster.

We arrived in the rendezvous area of route pack one and made contact with the FAC who had already stirred

Gen. Giraudo

up a hornets nest on the ground with some Gooks. The Misty FAC was glad to hear us check in since he was taking a lot of ground fire from the area that he was "working over" by himself. We very quickly got oriented, armed the bombs, and were ready for action.

The preparation and inflight briefing I gave to the rest of the flight was very quick. We rolled in, in the proper sequence so that not all would roll in on the same heading. Each came off the target in good shape and it looked like we destroyed the target the FAC had in mind so we all started to join up for recovery. Things were working just as briefed and planned. I was ready to return to Takhli for the last time with 100 missions under my belt and I was really damned happy. I couldn't believe how smooth this mission had gone.

All of a sudden, the relatively quiet frequency and silence was broken by "Misty" who was calling us for a request. He asked if we had the fuel and anymore ammo left because he was taking fire from one of the hills nearby where we bombed. He needed some help to put it out of commission. Well, we had the fuel since everything happened so fast and worked so smooth after we arrived in the area, and all four aircraft still had 20 millimeter (MM) gun ammo left.

We had already joined in route formation and were heading west out of North Vietnam on our way home. I thought I had finished my tour!

I had a choice and decision to make! I could ignore the request and keep pressing and be assured of actually returning home. I mean "Home", to family, the wife and kids, or return to the target area one more time as requested from a guy whose hurting and trying to do his job. He doesn't know I'm on my last mission and furthermore, that should not have anything to do with it anyway.

I knew what the unwritten rules were. Don't make second passes, and don't get into a 20 MM pissing contest with a gun sight because you usually lose and they win. The odds were usually against you. I always tried to comply with the tried and proven rules, but I also knew that you had to balance them against the immediate situation and then make a decision which best fits. We had the fuel and the ammo and after all, that's what we were here for. I couldn't refuse the request.

Since I had harped on these "no no's" during the briefing and hammered on them to Col Giraudo during previous missions, I knew he must be thinking what a hypocrite I was. I also knew, that he knew how I felt about returning to the target area, particularly on this mission after I'd dropped my bombs and supposedly finished with my 100.

I called Misty and told him we had some 20MM ammo and fuel and that we'd help. We turned around and headed back to the target area to see what "good ole" "Misty" had for us this time. We got directions to the flak sight that was causing him problems. I directed the flight to roll in in a specific order and had intended for one pass and then we'd leave. As it turned out, after we all made our strafing runs, we still hadn't silenced the guns so we were asked to make one more run. I thought, "what the hell", why not if we all have the ammo and fuel.

After I checked the fuel and ammo status of the rest of the flight, we still had more 20 MM left and the fuel for one more pass. I decided to give them one more parting shot. I knew we were really sticking our necks out now, and so far, we were very lucky or those NVN gunners were lousy shots. They were getting plenty of practice on us.

I decided to leave the area as though we were departing, and then return, hopefully, unexpectedly, make a very quick strafing run and leave. So we rejoined as a flight, left the area, then did a 180 turn and hit them one more time. On my last pass, and the last one of the war for me, I layed on the trigger and emptied the gun. The roar or hum of the gun is awesome when you hear it, even from the cockpit, and the damage it does is just as bad as it sounds. We all came off the target once again with no one taking hits and proceeded to join up for the last time, I hoped!

The FAC thanked us for the cooperation and said he thought we'd silence the guns. We couldn't help him any more anyway.

I was finished! Absolutely through! Out of ammo and ideas except to return to Takhli and finally HOME!

I was really happy! Many thoughts went through my mind at this point. The entire tour, the guys we'd lost, the frustrations, agony of completing this combat tour. I thought about the others, following me, that would have the same experiences, frustrations and maybe worse luck than I. At least I had finished 100 missions and was going home. I knew some would not, and had not been so lucky!

The return to Takhli, the 100 mission pass over the base, and celebration on the ramp after I parked was great!

After I cleared the runway and started to taxi in, fire trucks were there to meet and escort me in to the parking ramp as was the custom. As I taxied down the parallel taxiway back to the parking ramp, I unstrapped my shoulder harness, got out of my parachute and stood up in the cockpit, waving my arms and hands wildly while still taxiing. (I'd never done this before, ever, but I was overwhelmed with joy) I was so damned happy! I was actually crying with joy! Sirens were going off and the fire trucks had their red lights flashing! It was a great feeling and sight.

When I taxied onto the parking ramp to park, It dawned on me that this may be the last time I will fly the F-105. In fact I remember thinking, I probably won't see combat again unless I do a second tour. I've dropped my last bomb and fired the gun the last time.

I was being assigned back to the states to an F-106 assignment at the Air Defense Weapons Training Center in Florida and probably would not fly the F-105 again. I stopped short of parking for a few seconds to gather my thoughts since the Wing Commander (Col Giraudo), who had landed just minutes before, my Squadron C.O. (Col Norris), and a host of other guys were waiting to congratulate me on my completion of 100 missions. More importantly, I wanted to wait a second or two to look at the cockpit one more time. The F-105 had seen me through some tough times and I shall never forget her for pulling me through the damage I had taken on several missions.

I also knew that when I climbed down that ladder this time, I'd be leaving not only the F-105 but a lot of friends who still had not completed their missions and may never complete 100.

I was to leave for Bangkok in an hour. A C-47 was standing by at Base Ops waiting to take me to Bangkok. I'd only have a few minutes after I parked to pick up my belongings at my trailer before going to Base Operations where the C-47 was waiting. It would be a quick departure since I had already packed all my belongings (which wasn't much, only a B-4 Bag) before the mission. My 100 mission party was the night before at the O'Club since my departure was planned for an immediate departure after my 100th the next day.

After I parked, I got the routine congratulations and the 100 mission soak down with a fire hose of water and then we all shared some champagne right there at the airplane. I changed flying suits and proceeded to my trailer, picked up my B-4 bag and was taken to Base Ops by my good friend Jim Baldwin for departure to Bangkok. I'd be leaving for the States the next day from Bangkok on the earliest charter flight. I'd be leaving a lot of friends behind, not all of whom would be coming back.

The day before my 100th mission, I made a point of checking the Honor Roll board at Wing Headquarters to once more review the list of those who had been shot down and either were POWs, Missing (MIA), or Killed (KIA).

The Honor Roll listed the names of the pilots, the date shot down, and their status. I counted 41 during the time frame I was there (Feb 1 Thru 18 Aug '67). This did not count those who were fortunate enough to have been rescued after being shot down or any of the pilots in the sister F-105 Wing at Korat AB, Thailand further to the east of Takhli. The 388th TFW at Korat probably had about the same number of losses since they flew a similar number of missions each day to the same targets we did.

This had been a period of heavy losses for F-105s carrying the bombing to the north. I felt very lucky to have finished. I felt sorry for those who had not made it and for those who were still trying to complete their tour.

One of the reasons I wanted to leave as soon as possible after my last mission was the fear of how I would feel if I stayed around, even one more day knowing I was through and wouldn't have to sweat out any more missions while the rest of the wing pilots were still hard at it. I imagined the guilt feelings would be pretty strong if anyone was shot down during that time. I was feeling a little guilty about leaving. My emotions were mixed! I was happy to be alive and finished, but I felt guilty about not having to go back into the barrel again while all the others did. I needed out of there as quickly as possible now that I had finished.

*333 TFS Squadron group photon of Takhli flight line ramp in front of F-105 around March or April '67. Front Row L-R: Mike McCuistion; Capt. Earl Drew; Capt. Bill Lewis; Capt. Dave Cobb; Capt. "Buddy" Jones; Capt. Tom Lesan. Middle Row L-R: Lt. Ken Mathews; Capt. Farrington; Lt. Smith; Maj. Al Lenski; Lt/Col. Bill Norris (Sqd. C.O.); Lt/Col. Klobasa; Capt. Norm Frith; Capt. Gordon "Buz" Blackwood. Back Row L-R: Maj. Mike Tingelstad; Maj. Copeland; Maj. Carl Osborn; Maj. Bill Whealan; Maj. Ralph Kitchens; Capt. Layton; Maj. Ed Dobson.*

# Chapter Sixteen
# *"Returning Home"*

The adjustment period to a peacetime environment following this 100 mission combat tour is an experience which I shall never forget. Aside from the adjustment to peacetime living and association with wife, family, and mixed parties again, for a pilot who will continue flying in an active capacity in a peacetime role, the adjustment period is one that could be very dangerous.

There is a feeling of invincibility. That nothing could be as bad as flying 100 missions into route pack 6 as a Thud driver who survived. Overconfidence prevails to the point of being almost self destructive. Such were my feelings along with other invincibility feelings which seem to carry over into every facet of life. There was a saying in the Air Force among pilots who had orders to Southeast Asia in an F-105 when they screwed up and expected some sort of reprimand. It went something like this, " What are they going to do about it, give me a F-105 tour?" That kind of said it all.

As soon as I arrived in Bangkok from Takhli, the evening I finished my tour, I sent a telegram to Bettye, my wife, telling her I had completed my 100 missions and would be on the next plane back to San Francisco on the 20th. The plan was for Bettye to meet me in San Francisco where we'd spend a few days before returning to Wichita, Kansas and the kids. Bettye had either been expecting a telegram from me telling her I had completed 100 missions and returning home or an Air Force staff car with some bad news.

I felt great about having finished my tour and getting back home but nagging thoughts of Takhli and missions being flown by those still there kept flashing back to me. I kept looking at my watch to correlate the time to the activities that I knew should be going on at the Wing and Squadron. Depending on the time of day, I'd picture the preparation for missions, or where the strike force would be at any given moment during a pack 6 strike. It was constantly on my mind. I wondered which pack 6 target they were going to and whether any one was shot down and wondering if it was any close friends I knew. These were awful feelings, particularly that next morning and that first day away from combat.

Anyway, I kept thinking about the activities of the air war while on the airplane all the way back to the states. As the plane approached the west coast near San Francisco, I was amazed at how similar it looked to the jagged coast line in the Gulf of Tonkin off north Vietnam. Maybe I wanted it to look similar. I don't know, but I remember pretending it was and that certain little islands were good Initial Points (IPs) or Turn Points (TPs) for dead reckoning navigation to targets.

As the Golden Gate bridge came into view, I thought, "what a great target it would be to bomb". Then I could see dozens of "would be" targets to hit. Road and Railroad bridges, railroad yards and sidings, power plant facilities etc. I was really getting back into it again and here I was about to land and see my wife after 7 months, which seemed like an eternity, and I was still thinking war and bombing targets and there I was looking at the good ole USA.

Bearing in mind that it had only been the second day away from flying combat, I hadn't completely stopped thinking about it. Things were happening too quickly. Distances were shrinking rapidly. I really had not had time to adjust to not being in a combat role.

I couldn't believe that I was in a peacetime situation and not in an area affected by the bombing and the killing that went on only a couple days ago, several thousand miles away. For six months, it had been combat flying, everyday, bombing, and trying to survive. I just could not adjust that quick. I kept asking myself, how could things change so fast?

*Lt. Col. Jack Graber*

The initial shock came when I exited the airplane at San Francisco Airport and I entered the terminal. I don't know what I expected, but as I came through the jet bridge from the aircraft into the terminal area, I was amazed at all the people moving around in the terminal. I of course was looking for Bettye, really not knowing whether or not she was able to make it in time to meet me in San Francisco. It was so unlike where I had just come from. It just didn't seem like anyone knew that a war was going on in Vietnam. There was an aura of non concern. I could feel it. Like no one cared about what was happening over there. I had my short sleeve Khaki uniform on and looked like I was really out of place. I didn't like the feeling I had now that I was back in the States. Something seemed terribly wrong.

I finally saw Bettye coming towards me from about 20 yards away and I forgot all about the war. We had a great time in San Francisco for the next couple of days and then returned to McConnell AFB in Kansas. I had a great reunion with the kids and took a couple of weeks leave before we made our way to my new flying assignment in Florida.

The dangerous part for me was getting back to flying again with this feeling of overconfidence. Imagine, flying and not having to worry about someone shooting at you when that's all you've experienced for the last 7 months or so.

My first non-combat flight after returning to the States was in a T-33 with Jack Graber, a personal friend since my RF-101 days in Phalsbourg, France '60. Jack had also finished his 100 in the F-105 and was now an F-105 instructor at McConnell AFB. We flew from McConnell AFB, to Tyndall AFB in Panama City, Florida, my new assignment, where I did some house hunting.

I remember how simple it seemed to just prepare to fly. No Intelligence briefings, target study time, or reviewing the Air Order of Battle maps for enemy defenses. All we had to do is just file a flight plan clearance form and fly, and with no refueling either.

After getting airborne, I remember looking around all the time, particularly to the rear for Migs and being ever aware of any other airplanes nearby. I had quite an adjustment to get use to in peacetime flying again.

There would be no targets to bomb, no flak, no SAMs, or Migs attacking. Just fly from point A to B without having to use deadreckoning. Navigation facilities were again available the entire route. The only thing to worry about was an aircraft malfunction. Even if you had to eject, rescue was always available with everyone trying to help. Before this combat tour, I used to worry about having an anircraft malfunction which may cause me to have to eject. Now, however, I didn't mind it at all. If I had to eject, so what, I'm in the U.S., there was plenty of help available to recover me and ATC always knew where you were. There was no such thing as escape and evasion and safe areas to think about. Everyone on the ground would be trying to help, not hurt you. My whole mind set had changed.

This was "piece of cake" flying, unbelievable! The problem was that I would find myself taking more chances while flying now than I probably should. There was this feeling that I could press any situation to the maximum limits and nothing would happen to me.

The most lasting after effects of this combat tour for me, however, have been the dreams or nightmares that have occurred over these past 24 years (at this writing). In my dreams, I have relived so many of these missions. But the worst dream that seems to recur is the one which has me going back for another 100 missions. I don't know how many times I've had this same dream. Each time I get orders to go back for another F-105, 100 mission tour and I go back and fly it, reliving the experiences I remember so vividly each time, and I hate every minute of it.

I've not had one for awhile now, so maybe I'm coming to grips with the tour and all that it represented. I can only say in retrospect, that although this tour only lasted about 7 months, it was the most valuable, in spite of the fact that it was the most demanding and mentally difficult than any of the others in my 30 year Air Force career. I learned more about myself, about integrity, courage, and what a person is really made of than any other tour that I've had. For that, I am thankful.

## APPENDIX 1

*The following is a list of the 100 NVN, F-105 "Strike" missions flown during my tour in 1967.*

| NO. | DATE | TGT | COORD | PKG |
|-----|------|-----|-------|-----|
| 1. | 6 Feb | Rd brdg | 1827/10546 | 2 |
| 2. | 7 Feb | CP Rd cut | 1715/10652 | 1 |
| 3. | 13 Feb | Rd Brdg, Wrong tgt hit | 1640/10534 | Laos |
| 4. | | Rd Brdg and Rd | 1740/10630 | |
| 5. | 24 Feb | Rd cut | 1931/10358 | Laos |
| 6&7 | | Cp, Rd cut | | 1 |
| 8. | 2 Mar | CP, Rd cut | 1715/10652 | 1 |
| 9. | 4 Mar | Rd Brdg N of Dong Hoi | 1733/10633 | 1 |
| 10 | 20 Mar | Rd Cut (MuGia Pass) | 1744/10546 | 1 |
| 11 | | Laos, (5 Hr mission) | 1530/105XX | 1 |
| 12 | 21 Mar | Rd Brdg near Bat Lake | 1714/10643 | 1 |
| 13 | 22 Mar | Rd Trucks (MuGia Pass) | 1753/10549 | 1 |
| 14 | 23 Mar | Rd Brdg near Bat Lake | 1714/10643 | 1 |
| 15 | 28 Mar | Rd Brdg | 1754/10622 | 1 |

| NO. | DATE | TGT | COORD | PKG |
|-----|------|-----|-------|-----|
| 16 | 28 Mar | Troops in cave | 2146/10340 | 5 |
| 17 | 29 Mar | RR-Rd on Route 7 | 1927/10408 | 2 |
| 18 | 30 Mar | RR-Rd Brdg | 2020/10419 | Laos |
| 19 | 31 Mar | Dong Hoi oil tanks etc. | 1727/10640 | 1 |
| 20 | 3 Apr | CP Troops and storage (Dien Bien Phu) | 2125/10305 | 5 |
| 21 | 3 Apr | CP Troops and storage (Dien Bien Phu) | 2125/10305 | 5 |
| 22 | 7 Apr | Ferry | 1752/10628 | 1 |
| 23 | 8 Apr | CP Troops and storage (Dien Bien Phu) | 2120/103 | 5 |
| 24 | 9 Apr | Rd Brdg | 1723/10542 | Laos |
| 25--29 | | Lower Route Packs | | |
| 30 | 18 Apr | Rd Cut | 1710/10604 | Laos |
| 31 | 26 Apr | Hanoi Thermal Pwr.Plant, | | 6 |
| | | (10 Mi N, Hanoi, JCS TGT) | | |
| 32 | | Lower Route Pack | | |
| 33 | 29 Apr | Troops/Ammo Ban Bang Storage | 1924/10306 | Laos |
| 34 | 30 Apr | Tgt Thermal Pwr Plant, Thorsness | 2118/10458 | 6 |
| | | (This mission covered in Thud Ridge" Book, | | |
| | | Longest Mission Chapter and "Going | | |
| | | Downtown,The War Against Hanoi | | |
| | | and Washington") | | |
| 35 | 3 May | Bac Ninh Rd/RR Bridg | 2110/10604 | 6 |
| 36 | 4 May | Same as 24 Lower Pack | | Laos |
| 37, 38 | | Lower Route Packs | | |
| 39 | 8 May | MuGia Pass, McCuiston Rescue unsuccessful, | | 1 |
| | | captured N of MuGia, -POW. | | |
| 40--47 | | Lower Route Packs | | |
| 48 | 20 May | Bac Le R/R siding near Kep (NE RR), | 2131/10626 | 6 |
| | | (Covered in USAF Aces book) | | |
| 49 | 21 May | MuGia Pass | 1759/10550 | 1 |
| 50 | 27 May | Bac Giang Rd/RR Brdg | | 6 |
| | | (Roomy, Blackwood down) MIA/KIA | | |
| 51 | | Lower Route Pack | | |
| 52 | 2 Jun | RR Siding NE R/R | 2115/10607 | 6 |
| 53--55 | | Lower Route Packs | | |
| 56 | 10 Jun | Thai Nguyen | | 6 |
| 57 | 17-Jun | Abort--stick locked on T/O, breaking ground. | (NO Counter) | |
| | | (Pliers in stick well) | | |
| 57 | 18 Jun | Thai Nguyen | | 6 |

| NO. | DATE | TGT | COORD | PKG |
|-----|------|-----|-------|-----|
| 58 | 19 Jun | Bac Giang RR Bridg | | 6 |
| 59 | 20 Jun | Phu Tho, Fertilizer Plant | | 6 |
| 60 | 21 Jun | Kep RR Yard | | 6 |
| 61 | 22 Jun | Thai Nguyen, Army Barracks, HIT on Thud Ridge | | 6 |
| 62 | 23 Jun | Rd/Ferry | 1830/10524 | 2 |
| 63 | 24 Jun | Rd Storage | 2015/10355 | Laos |
| 64 | 25 Jun | Rd Brdg | 1910/10537 | 3 |
| 65 | 27 Jun | Phu Tho Rd | | 6 |
| 66 | 28 Jun | Thon Nieu R/R Siding | 2131/10553 | 6 |
| 67 | 29 Jun | RR Tunnel | 2127/10611 | 6 |
| 68 | 30 Jun | RR Siding (Phuc Yen) | | 6 |
| 69 | 1 Jul | Rd Ferry | 2145/10503 | 6 |
| 70 | 3 Jul | Thai Nguyen | | 6 |
| 71 | 4 Jul | RR Tunnel | 2136/106 | 6 |
| 72 | 5 Jul | RR Tunnel | 2134/10610 | 6 |
| 73, 74 | | Lower Route Packs | | 1 |
| 75 | 12 Jul | RR Siding | 2133/10552 | 6 |
| 76 | 13 Jul | RR Siding | 2120/10553 | 6 |
| 77 | 15 Jul | RR Bridg | 1740/10622 | 1 |
| 78 | | Lower Route Pack | | |
| 79 | 18 Jul. | Same as 72 | | 6 |
| 80 | 19 Jul | Kep RR Siding | | 6 |
| 81 | 20 Jul | Yen-Bai, New Airfield construction | 2144/10452 | 6 |
| 82 | 21 Jul | Same as 72 | | 6 |
| 83 | 22 Jul | Lower Route Pack | | |
| 84 | 23 Jul | Rd Brdg out side Phuc Yen | | 6 |
| 85, 86 | | Lower Route Packs | | |
| 87 | 31 Jul | Kep RR Yard | | 6 |
| 88 | 2 Aug | Thai Nguyen (Ammo Storage) | | 6 |
| 89 | 3 Aug | RR Tunnel, Same as 67 | | 6 |
| 90 | 4 Aug | RR Siding (Golden Rule extended to 95) | 2130/10554 | 6 |
| 91 | 5 Aug | Kep RR Yard | | 6 |
| 92-94 | | Lower Route Packs | | |
| 95 | 9 Aug | Vinh Yen RR Yard (NW Phuc Yen) | | 6 |
| 96-99 | | Finally Golden (Lower Route Packs) | | |
| 100 | Aug 18 | MuGia Pass, Magic 100 , Going Home! | | 1 |

# Glossary of Terms and Abbreviations

AAA—Antiaircraft artillery

AB—Afterburner (with respect to jet aircraft, see definition below): Air Base (with respect to an installation)

"Advanced flying training"—After "Basic" flying school and receiving pilot wings, the pilot was assigned to advanced flight training (usually 3 months) to specialize in the training on a specific aircraft type which had a specific type mission, i. e., all weather Interceptor, day fighter (Air-to-Air, or Air-to-Ground), Bomber, etc.; Following this training the pilot was then qualified to be assigned to active flying duty with a Combat Ready Squadron

Afterburner—An auxiliary burner attached to the tail pipe of a jet engine for injecting fuel into the hot exhaust gases and burning it to provide extra thrust

AGM-45—Shrike air-to-ground missile, anti-radiation type

AIM—Air-intercept missile

AIM-9—Sidewinder air-to-air missile, passive IR type (B, D, E, G, and J models) and radar-guided (C model)

Air abort—Cancellation of an aircraft mission for any reason other than enemy action, at any time from take-off to mission completion

AI radar—Airborne intercept radar

ATOLL—Soviet-built air-to-air missile, infrared seeker type, similar to U.S. AIM-9 IR-homing missile

Attach—To place units or personnel in an organization where such placement is relatively temporary

Ballistic—Unguided, i.e. follows a ballistic trajectory when thrust is terminated

Basic pilot training—A continuation of pilot training following Primary pilot training; This training was specialized into either fighter or bomber type aircraft of six more months and 120 hrs of instructional and solo flying time; In '53 the fighter training was split into about 60 hrs of T-28 (conventional engine) time and 60 hrs of initial jet training in a T-33/F-80 single engine aircraft; Following the successfull completion of this training the candidate received his pilot wings and was assigned to "Advanced flying training" in a specific aircraft type and mission

Bingo (fuel)— Minimum fuel quantity reserve established for a given geographical point to permit aircraft to return safely to its home base, an alternate base, or an aerial refueling point

Blip (radar)—A spot of light on a radar scope, representing the relative position of a reflecting object such as an aircraft; sometimes called "pip"

Bogey—Unidentified aircraft

Break (Broke)—An emergency turn in which maximum performance is desired instantly to destroy an attacker's tracking solution

"Burner"—Afterburner

CAP—Combat air patrol; an aircraft patrol provided over an objective area, over the force protected, over the critical area of a combat zone, or over an air defense area, for the purpose of intercepting and destroying hostile aircraft before they reach their target (See BARCAP, MIGCAP, RESCAP)

Cell(s)—Cellular unit(s) of airborne military aircraft, usually bombers and/or tankers, made up of a number of individually organized cells or teams which may operate independently of one another to provide flexibility

Centerline tank—A fuel tank carried externally on the centerline of the aircraft

Chatter (radio)—Multiple communications on the same radio frequency, usually applied to communications which are of little interest to the individual using the term

Close—To decrease separation between aircraft

Closure— Relative closing velocity

Col—Colonel

Cover-—The protection given to a surface area or force, or to a force of aircraft in the air, by maintaining fighter aircraft in the air to repel or divert attack, especially air attack; also, the aircraft providing, or designated to provide the protection

Crown—Voice call sign for the Rescue coordinator (usually an airborne C-130 aircraft)

Deck—A flight altitude just above the surface, as used in such phases as "to hit the deck," "to fly on the deck," and "to dive toward the deck"

Disengage—To break off combat with the enemy

DME—Distance measuring equipment

DMZ—Demilitarized zone

Dogfight—An aerial battle, especially between opposing fighters involving considerable maneuvering and violent aerobatics on both sides

"Drop off"—Term referring to refueling aircraft departing from the refueling tanker

EB-66—A light reconnaissance bomber which has several configurations for gathering electronic intelligence data or for radiating jamming to provide protection for strike forces

Echelon—A formation in which flight members are positioned sequentially on one side of the lead aircraft

ECM—Electronic countermeasures: the prevention or reduction of effectiveness in enemy equipment and tactics used by electromagnetic radiation's; some activities exploit the enemy's emissions of these radiation's

ECM pod—Pylon or fuselage-mounted container which houses multiple transmitters and associated electronic devices; self-protection device for aircraft penetrating an electronically-controlled ground-to-air defense system

Element—USAF item for the basic fighting unit (two aircraft)

Encounter— A series of time-continuous actions between specific US and enemy (or bogey) aircraft

Engagement—An encounter which involves hostile, or aggressive action by one or more of the participants

Envelope—A volume of airspace within which a particular weapon or weapon system must operate, be expended, or be employed in order to achieve maximum effectiveness; also field of maneuver

EWO—Electronic warfare officer

FAC—Forward air controller

Fast-Fac—A forward air controller in an F-100, F-4, or other fighter aircraft

Fingertip—A four-aircraft formation in which the aircraft occupy positions suggested by the four fingertips of either hand, the fingers being held together in a horizontal plane

1st Lt (or 1Lt) —Military rank of First Lieutenant

Flak—Antiaircraft shrapnel (usually from 37, 57, and larger caliber of AAA)

Flak envelope—A varying vertical unit of airspace in which a particular type of AAA is effective (See Envelope)

Flak suppression (Flight)—A term used to designate a specific task during a strike; The task is to "suppress" or destroy any Flak sites in and around the assigned target that are firing at the bombing aircraft with the weapons load carried . Normally a specific flight is designated to perform "Flak suppression" for the rest of the strike force or other flight members.

Flame(d) out—The extinguishment of the flame in a reaction engine, especially a jet engine

Flight—USAF term for a tactical fighter unit; when used in reference to aircraft, usually consisting of two elements, each element of two aircraft: when used in reference to a "Squadron unit", usually made of several "Flights" of pilots/navigators

Flight integrity—Aircraft maneuvering in relation to, and in support of, one another

FOD—Foreign-object-damage; Refers to the ingestion of an object into a jet engine through the open air intake(s); Substantial damage may occur causing a range of engine problems, from reduced thrust or flame-out to complete destruction

Frag—or Frag Order—A fragmentary operations order; the daily supplement to standard operations orders governing the conduct of the air war in Southeast Asia; directs a specific military mission

Fragged—Mission directed by fragmentary operational order from higher headquarters

Friendly (ies)—Aircraft belong to, or held by, one's own forces or the forces of an allied nation

G(s)—Unit of acceleration (32.2 ft/sec$^2$): unit of force applied to a body at rest equal to the force exerted on it by gravity

GCI—Ground-controlled intercept

Gen—Abbreviation for General, often in combination with other abbreviations for different levels, e.g., Brig (Brigadier) Gen, Maj Gen, or Lt Gen

G-load—The force exerted upon a pilot (and his aircraft) by gravity or a reaction to acceleration or deceleration as in a change of direction (maneuvering)

Guard—Emergency UHF radio channel usually monitored by all aircraft and ground stations as a secondary frequency, in addition to primary tactical frequencies

Guide—With respect to an air-to-air missile: to follow the course intended when fired

Hard turn—A planned turn in which the intensity of the turn is governed by the angle-off and range of the attacking aircraft

Home(d)—Of a missile: to direct itself toward the target by guiding on heat waves, radar, echoes, radio waves, or other radiation emanating from the target

IAS—Indicated air speed

IP—Initial point; a well-defined point, usually distinguishable visually and/or by radar, used as a starting point for a bomb run to a target or for other tactical purposes, such as air refueling

IR—Infrared

IR missile—An infrared (heat-seeking) missile

Iron Hand—Nickname for a flight with special ordnance and avionics equipment, with a mission of seeking and destroying enemy SAM sites and radar-controlled AAA sites

JCS—Joint Chiefs of Staff

JCS target—A target appearing on the JCS target list

Jink (ed) (ing)—Constant maneuvering in both the horizontal and vertical planes to present a difficult target to enemy defenses by spoiling the tracking solution; a simultaneous change in bank, pitch, and velocity—at random

Kill—An enemy airplane shot down or otherwise destroyed by military action while in flight

Kt—Knot (one nautical mile per hour)

Lead—The lead aircraft in a flight or element, or the lead element of a flight; also a reference to a specific lead aircraft or its pilot

Lethal envelope—The envelope within which parameters can be met for successful employment of a munition by a particular weapon system (See Envelope)

Lock-on—To follow a target automatically in one or more dimensions (e.g., range, bearing, elevation) by means of a radar beam

LtC—Lieutenant Colonel

M—Mach

Mach—The ratio of the aircraft's velocity to the velocity of sound in the surrounding medium

Maj—Major

Maximum power—Afterburner power

mi—Mile

MIG—The name for the Mikoyan/Gurevich series of Soviet jet fighter aircraft

MIGCAP (or MIG cap)—Combat air patrol directed specifically against MIG aircraft (See CAP)

mil—Milliradian; one mil=0.0573 degrees; one degree-17.45 mils; about one foot at 1,000 feet

Military power—Maximum unaugmented (no afterburner) thrust of the aircraft engine

mm—Millimeter, as in 20-mm, 37-mm, etc.

M-61—Vulcan 20-mm cannon used on the F-105 and F-4 aircraft

NAVAIDS—Navigational aids

Noise—Unwanted sound or disturbances found in or introduced into a communication system, or appearing on a radar scope

NVN—North Vietnam

Orbit—A circular or elliptical pattern flown by aircraft to remain in a specified area

Overshoot—To pass through the defender's flight path in the plane of symmetry

Overtake velocity or speed—Sudden gain in speed to come up on another aircraft

PACAF—Pacific Air Forces

Peeled off—To roll the aircraft away from its original flight path; usually away from other aircraft in the formation

Pickle(ed)—Term used referring to the act of causing the release or firing of the selected weapons carried on board the aircraft; In case of most fighter aircraft, a red colored "Pickle" button on the control stick grip, when depressed, released bombs or fired missiles, as selected on the weapons control panel in the cockpit

Pipper—A 2-mil diameter dot in the center of the optical sight reticle (gunsight)—a dot of light within a lighted ring—used for aiming

Pod—Any one of several aerodynamically configured subsystems carried externally on fighter aircraft

Pod formation—A formation of two or more aircraft flown in such a way that ECM pods installed on each aircraft offer mutual and maximum protection

Pop-up (maneuver)—A climbing maneuver from a low-altitude position or other position of concealment, used to gain an advantageous position for weapons delivery; also a maneuver used by enemy aircraft which involved a steep climb from a low-altitude area of concealment to an inbound aircraft or flight of aircraft

"Primary" pilot training—Entry level pilot training; In '52, this was six months with 120 hrs instructional and solo flying time in a T-6 type aircraft

Pull-up—An act or instance of pulling up; a pullout, or recovery from a dive; to bring the nose of an aircraft up sharply, especially from a level attitude

Pylon—A projection under an aircraft's wing, designed for suspending ordnance, fuel tanks or pods

QRC-160—Quick reaction capability noise jamming ECM pod, developed to counter new radar threats

Recce—Reconnaissance

Recon—Reconnaissance

Red Crown—Voice call sign for the radar-equipped USS Long Beach (CLN-9), the USN's PIRAZ ship, stationed in the northern part of the Gulf of Tonkin, which performed GCI functions

RESCAP—Rescue combat air patrol (See CAP)

RHAW—Radar homing and warning; on-board aircraft equipment to warn pilot of active enemy defenses

Roger—Term meaning "Message received and understood"

Roll(ed) in—The initial act of rolling the aircraft into a diving position for a dive bomb or strafe attack to launch weapons at a ground target or an aircraft

Rolling Thunder—Nickname for JCS-directed USAF air strikes against targets in North Vietnam; began as gradual reprisals rather than hard-hitting military campaigns, but gradually escalated into major air strikes as the war continued; phases of Rolling Thunder: Phase I, 2 Mar-11 May 1965; Phase II, 18 May-24 Dec 1965; Phase III, 31 Jan-31 Mar 1966; Phase IV, 1 Apr-24 Dec 1966; Phase V, 14 Feb-24 Dec 1967; and Phase VI, 3 Jan-1 Nov 1968

Rollout—Termination of a maneuver, or series of maneuvers, designed to place an aircraft in a position which would most optimally assure completion of the intended activity, e.g., airborne intercept, instrument approach

Route Package—One of seven geographical divisions of North Vietnam assigned for air strike targeting (RP 1 through 5, 6A, and 6B); Roman numerals sometimes used rather than Arabic, such as RP-6A (See map, p. i)

RP—(See Route Package)

RTAFB—Royal Thai Air Force Base

RTB—Return (ed) to base

Ruddered—(See YAW) Term meaning to use the aircraft's rudders to move the aircraft laterally without other flight control inputs (aileron or elevator) which causes the aircraft to skid about the lateral axis in an un-coordinated maneuver

SAM—Surface-to-air missile (SA-2-Soviet-built surface-to-air missile system)

Sandwich—Situation wherein an aircraft is positioned between two opposing aircraft

SAR—Search and rescue

SEA—Southeast Asia

Separation—The distance between the interceptor and the target aircraft; can be lateral, longitudinal, or vertical

Separation maneuver—An energy-gaining maneuver performed with a low angle of attack and maximum thrust, to increase separation (extend) or decrease separation (close)

Shrike—Nickname for the AGM-45 air-to-ground radar-seeking missile

"S"-ing, "S" maneuver—Performing a series of "S" turns. A weave in a horizontal plane

Six—Six (6) o'clock position or area; refers to the rear of aft area of an aircraft

Speedbrakes—Flaps designed for slowing down an aircraft in flight

Squadron Officer School—The entry level of several Air Force professional military education schools within the Air Force's "Air University" located at Maxwell AFB, Alabama, designed for junior (1st Lt. and Captains) officers

Strafe(ing)—To rake with a machine-gun (20mm cannon) fire from low-flying aircraft, normally at close range

Strike(s)—An attack upon a surface target, intended to inflict damage on or to destroy an enemy objective

Strike Force—More than one flight of bomber aircraft along with its MigCap which are assigned to strike targets. Normally the strike force to package 6 (Hanoi area) consisted of four bombing flights of 4 F-105 aircraft each, one F-105 flight of 4 weasel (SAM suppression) and one or two flights of four F-4 MigCap aircraft

Sweep—An offensive mission by several fighter aircraft, sometimes accompanied by fighter-bombers, over a particular area of enemy territory for the purpose of seeking out and attacking enemy aircraft or targets of opportunity; the action of flying over an area in making a search; the path flown in making a search; to clear the skies or other places of opposition

TAC—Tactical Air Command

TACAN-Tactical air navigation; an active electronic navigational system which locates the aircraft with respect to another installation

TDY—Temporary duty; the status of being on TDY

Tet—Vietnamese lunar New Year

TFS—Tactical fighter squadron

TFW—Tactical fighter wing

Thud—Nickname for the F-105

Thud Ridge—Nicknamed after the many F-105s that used this mountain range for navigational and terrain masking and the many that were shot down in this area during strike force operations. Located in RP-6A, beginning about 20NM north-northwest of Hanoi and extending about 25 NM northwest.

TOT—Time over target

Tracking—Term referring to the maintaining of the center of the field of view of search radars or airborne sensors on a target

Trail formation—Aircraft directly behind one another

Troll(ed)(ing)—Flying a random pattern by ECM aircraft to detect enemy electronic signals; flying a pattern in a specific area to detect signals of a suspected SAM or AAA site

Turn radius—A radial distance required to effect a 180 degree turn which varies according to the aircrafts speed and altitude

Turn Point(TP)—a well-defined point, usually distinguishable visually and/or by radar, used as a starting point for a bomb run to a target or for other tactical purposes (Also see IP)

UHF(Radio)—Ultra high frequency (Radio communication equipment using UHF)

USAF—United States Air Force

Weapons system—Refers to the combination of aircraft, crew, ordnance, avionics, etc.

Weave—A formation in which the two elements of a flight or the two members of an element continuously cross each other's flight path, normally in the horizontal plane, to increase their visual coverage of each other's rear area; also provides a difficult tracking problem for ground radar's or enemy guns

Wild Weasel—F-105F aircraft equipped with RHAW and anti-radiation missiles, enabling them to home on SA-2 radar guidance signals and to mark the location of missile sites

Wingman—Pilot (or aircraft) who flies at the side and to the rear of an element leader. In an aircraft flight, 02 is wingman to lead (01), and 04 is wingman to 03. Usually, more experienced pilots fly the lead and 03 positions in a flight, and these pilots initiate combat actions while their wingmen fly cover

WSO—Weapon systems officer; backseater in the two seated (Weasel) F-105 or F-4

Yaw—Rotation of an aircraft about its vertical axis so as to cause the longitudinal axis of the aircraft to deviate from the line of flight

# PEOPLE INDEX

An F-105 taken by the boom operator of a KC-135. (Courtesy of David Waldrop.)

9 781681 623191